NO
SIGHT
NO
TASTE
NO
SOUND
NO
TOUCH
NO
SMELL

WHAT BOOK!?

BUDDHA
POEMS
FROM
BEAT
TO
HIPHOP

Edited by
GARY GACH

Foreword by
PETER COYOTE

PARALLAX PRESS
BERKELEY, CALIFORNIA

Parallax Press
P.O. Box 7355
Berkeley, California 94707

Cover and text design by Legacy Media, Inc.
Cover painting, *He,* by Don Martin (1969). Used with permission of Joan
Martin. The painting reproduced on the cover of this book began as sprayed
enamel paint on plywood, torched to blister and peel, then completed with
acrylic.
Photograph of cover art by Tony Grant.

LIBRARY OF CONGRESS CATALOGING-IN-PUBLICATION DATA

What book!? : Buddha poems from beat to hiphop / edited by Gary Gach :
    foreword by Peter Coyote.
        p.   cm.
    Includes index.
    ISBN 0-938077-92-9
    1. Buddhist poetry, American. 2. American poetry—20th century.
I. Gach, Gary.
PS595.B83W47   1998   98-5403
811' .54080382—dc21   CIP

1 2 3 4 5 6 7 8 9 10 / 02 01 00 99 98

CONTENTS

FOREWORD

PETER COYOTE

Some years ago I began noticing alternative archetypes to the American Eagle surfacing in *tchotchke* shops and galleries wherever I traveled. Owls were first: cookie jars, ticking clocks where the eyes moved left and right, bookends, posters, pigeon-chasers to mount on the roof, and lawn decorations. Soon after that initial perception crystallized, Coyotes began to intrude as well: lawn decorations, lamps, photos, tin-prints, and the same paraphernalia dedicated to Owl. Contemporary with that perception a vogue of chile restaurants spawned like mushrooms, and menus began to litanize Aztec and Nahuatl words filtered through Spanish, like *chipotle, jalapeño,* and *habañero*. It was inescapable. The continent was beginning to assert itself through the popular imagination and the five senses.

Something of the same phenomenon is occurring with Buddhism. This gentlest of all practices, based on perceptions sharpened by meditation, is beginning to capture a population no longer sustained by Judeo-Christian archetypes and dichotomized, comparative thinking. Hollywood moguls sport Tibetan thangkas on office walls; benefits for Tibetan refugees and the Dalai Lama are ubiquitous; the Bay Area where I live has at least five Zen centers and many more centers in other traditions of Buddhism.

The "antennae of the race," according to Ezra Pound's description of the artist, have been in the forefront of this trans-mutation, beginning with the Transcendentalists and contin-uing with the Beat poets in the late forties and fifties. Poets like Gary Snyder, Allen Ginsberg (a deep *gassho* to his memory), Philip Whalen, Jack Kerouac, Bob Kaufman, and Robert Duncan first brought the message of traceless interpenetra-tions from the sacred texts into the realm of uttered discourse in a popular context, and, as they should be, they are well rep-resented in these pages. Zen masters and practitioners like Nyogen Senzaki, Suzuki Roshi, Robert Aitken, Kazuaki Tanahashi, John Tarrant, Steve Sanfield, Mel Weitsman, Bernard

Tetsugen Glassman, Master Seung Sahn, and Taizan Maezumi Roshi, have continued the ancient poetic traditions of Buddhist culture and added their rivulets to the swelling waters of Buddhist expression in America. Contemporaries like Scoop Nisker (a local Bay Area disc jockey) and author Jim Harrison join Jane Hirshfield, Anne Waldman, Garrett Hongo, Maxine Hong Kingston, and Lawson Fusao Inada, and as I continue to type I am forced to leave the paltry metaphor of creeks and streams and begin to consider the more appropriate scale of rivers and oceans as more suitable to express the scale and imprint of Buddhism on contemporary culture.

Easily half of the extensive list of contributors in this book are either friends, comrades, fellow Zen students, or teachers of mine. Seeing them all gathered in one place gladdens the heart and makes me feel as if I have been catapulted into deep space and am now able to look down on the Earth from on-high and truly appreciate the scale of Buddhism's hold on the popular mind. If there were an appropriate color for Buddhism, it would have to be non-color transparency, and from my new perspective, the atmosphere itself, cradling our gem-like planet floating in darkest void represents the spread and pressure of Buddhism on every continent. It is ubiquitous, colorless, odorless (generally), and irrevocably there. These poems are the pointing finger and the target; the moon and its reflection in a puddle. They are inhalation and exhalation; tiny Dharma sandwiches. Finger food for the spiritually hungry. How lucky we are to be invited to attend this banquet. I give three deep bows to all the chefs and a special one to editor Gary Gach, our maitre d' who has organized this splendid, empty feast. I can't wait to get at it, but in the immortal words of Kwan Yin, "After you."

Peter Coyote
May 1997

Welcome to the calm, clear, everyday wonderland of mindful poetry.

About this book

Here are contemporary intersections of poetry and meditation, from many fascinating diverse directions.

All attesting to how many paths there are to Buddha. To mindfulness. Buddha and mindfulness being of the same nature.

Mindful poetry. Being aware. Attentive. Mindful of what we need to live.

What Book!? is an instance of the range of that human possibility.

A gathering, in order to then step back to see how it all looks together. As on a big corkboard. Or an unfolding scroll.

With only that as its initial intention, rather than any preset idea to flesh out, this book truly took on an organic shape of its own, the way a marathon poetry reading or slam* unfolds; a festival.

I defined "from Beat to Hiphop" more as a range of time than as emphasizing any particular style. Though I did not strive to be definitive in my selection, each poem, text, or excerpt has its unique reason for being here. Thematic elements emerged from the wealth of materials that I discovered, serving as guides, not so much as distinct categories but more often resonating with each other, forming harmonic chords. I've posted my own commentary, along with additional poems, on the World-Wide Web.** But the finger pointing at the moon is not the moon. Be assured this assembling will transport you, in and of itself, without need of explanation.

Anyway, here's a brief preview. At the bottom of the page you'll see little trail-markers. That's all they are. Feel free to

---

* Slam: A competition of performance poetry, with judges in the audience.

** http://word.to/whatweb.html

disagree with the labels, or ignore them. Literature is, after all, a dialogue.

This book starts and ends with a prelude and a coda, but it's all been going on before this book began and continues on well after we're gone. So "No Beginning No End." And each of these sections contains the others.

"Original Mind" acknowledges both that essential identity of which we all partake, and some of the original minds who originally woke many of us up through their poetry.

"Beatific" alludes both to the Beat Generation and illumination, bliss.

"You, Everywhere" speaks of passion both spiritual and bodily, human and divine.

"Kindred" groups various voices from a common background.

"Family and Friends" deals with Sangha, the Buddhist community that lives in harmony and awareness. You'll find the horizons here expanded to include parents, kids, teachers, ancestors, monks, and ravens.

"Bearing Witness" alludes to another Buddhist concept, summed up as nonjudgmental, compassionate, deep listening. Hearing the story of another as one's own. A way of acceptance. Healing.

"Guides Along the Path" pays further homage to trailblazers.

"Flower, Fresh" offers a number of strategies for becoming aware of the is-ness, now-ness, and such-ness of being. Ways of seeing miracles as no different than everyday life.

"Make It New" reflects the influence of Buddhism and mindfulness on twentieth-century culture: such as field composition (poetry free of meter and rhyme), conceptual art, performance art, etc.

"Visible Language" takes that ball and runs with it, to wild, wide open spaces. The spell of language as play. The very process and activity of writing (and reading and hearing) can wake us up. Words themselves are Buddhas.

There is a tranquility that comes from seeing things as they are. "Calm, Ease." Poems coming from peace can bring us there through the simplest of means. Poetry is less words than prose, and Zen* poetry can be even less than that.

* "Zen" in Japan, "Ch'an" in China, "Son" in Korea, "Thien" in Vietnam – all mean meditation. ("We teach ourselves. Zen merely points the way." – D. T. Suzuki.)

"Teachings" refers both to the Dharma, Buddha's teachings, the path of understanding and love – and, also, yet again to trailblazing guides along that path.

The next two signposts are "Silence" and "Song." Where the Western mind-set sees contradiction between the two, the Buddhist mind sees relationship, interrelatedness.

It is said that Buddha once taught his disciples by only holding up a flower and smiling. *No words.*

The monk Mahakashyapa saw the flower, really saw it, got it, and smiled.

And without silence there'd be no words. No music – that beautiful thing. Poetry's upper limits are defined by song.

After silence and song, what else is there to be said but perhaps offer a bouquet of flowers? To Buddha.

Buddha is the one who shows us the way in this life. Whoever or whatever awakens us to be aware of life all around us. "Toward Buddha" gathers poems dedicated to that: many are by Zen masters, from Zen ritual, rich in metaphor.

And we awaken to our true nature and nature all around, at the same time. You don't have to be Buddhist to appreciate the wonder and power of nature, be it mountain or river, cherry blossom or hickory. I call the marker here "Nature, the Teacher" after a Zen adage: "It is nature alone that teaches us about itself."

As a bonus, Allen Ginsberg (a deep bow to his memory) generously gives us a collection of mind writing slogans and exercises. And, as a capper, a meditation by Thich Nhat Hanh.

Poetry & mindfulness

This book puts the reins of poetry and life in your hands. The voice of the Buddha recalling us to the source, to our finest impulse, to our true home, in the present moment – akin to the voice of the bard.

A poet once located poetry as somewhere before or after words take place. Mindfulness is the practice of finding that realm. Dwelling there. Cultivating the ability to live completely in the present. Deeply aware and appreciative of life.

Mindfulness is at the heart of Buddhist meditation; is, you might say, the energy of Buddha. In Chinese, the word "mindfulness" is a composite: the character for "now" is drawn above the character for "mind" – which is traditionally the picture of a heart, implying body and mind united.

Open mind, open heart. Reflecting what is real, true, and beautiful. It is an *art*.

Mindfulness,
touching peace;
being peace.
Poetry,
    singing peace;
    bringing peace.
Poetry and mindfulness intertwine; interact; interreact.

A book of mindful poetry probably won't stop war. Violence. Hysteria. Fear.

And yet ...

A single wild iris blooming on a city hillside or faintly quivering in a vase at an altar can be enough.

Readers wishing to delve even more deeply into engaged Buddhism are invited to select a book from the publisher's copious catalogue. For example, *Being Peace*.

So let's turn the spotlight on poetry now, in the context of mindfulness.

Many if not most of these poems inherit a tradition that's been absent of late, once called devotional poetry. Sermon. Prayer. Meditation.

Until the technological revolution, poetry and the sacred were as close as ember and coal. But awareness of tide, wind, and seed became preempted by watt, volt, and amp; earth's six-cycle-per-second hum muted by electricity's sixty-cycle-per-second strobe. Yet the impulse for reverence endures.

Reclaiming the sacred in our lives naturally brings us close once more to the wellsprings of poetry. For instance, it's now commonplace for American churches to hold open-mike poetry readings, acknowledging the unity of culture and faith.

Who hasn't been inspired by the sheer poetry of sacred texts?

And what sacred text isn't informed by poetry? That is, when Jesus, Lao-tze, Moses, Plato, Mohammed, the Buddha spoke – as they speak to us today – their language of address is poetry. To be grasped – understood, followed – as we would a poem.

Poetry reveals energies we need in order to live. Different energies are revealed by different forms. There is no one model for a "Buddhist poem."

Western poets have been influenced by Eastern forms, such as *haiku* and *tanka* (short Japanese poetry), *koans* (riddles pointing to the nature of ultimate reality) and *gathas* (short poems for meditation), plus shamanic spells (for care of the earth, against demons, or for healing), augury, folk song, etc.

There are Eastern meditative origins of Western forms, too. Consider the quatrain. In a classical Chinese quatrain, the first line proposes something, the second line continues it, the third advances something seemingly different, and the fourth unites and brings it all back home. (The quatrain *turns* on the third line. The word "verse" means "turning.")

Any poem wants to be read more than once or twice. To become embodied and clear in your mind's eye.

Try this: Read a poem once by eye, silently. Then again by ear, aloud to yourself. Then read it through once more.

Haiku, for example, are one-breath long.

A breathing room. An invitation to listen not only to what is said but what is unsaid too.

And rhyme, if it occurs, maps the melody.

The song the mute heart feels, moving through this world.

It is easy to lose the sacred power of words through their sheer abundance in newspaper, radio, TV, movie, phone, fax, voice mail, e-mail, etc. Poetry is a reminder. Slow down. Enjoy the flowers along the way.

Poetry may seem to be only prose cut into short lines
– but at the end of each line lets us breathe, be attentive –
as if we could get up, walk around the block, and come
back, to continue the next line
renewed, without missing a stitch –
or spend five minutes on a single line, if need be.

So take time. Make space, for the chance that poetry can take place in your life. Every day. Moment to moment.

Dreams "come true" in poetry. Just as a wild iris grows on a city hill slope. Seen just as it is.

Open the eye within the eye. The heart within the heart. Lighten the life you live and the lives around you.

The Korean poet Ko Un, when reading with Gary Snyder at Black Oak Books in Berkeley, told the audience: "To me, poetry is being here with you."

We write most mindfully when aware of our breathing, our mind, eye, and hands, writing, all at once.

And much the same is true for reading.

Thus poetry calls for mindful readers, as well as writers.

Enjoy the journey. Come and go as you please. The poetry will still be going on when you get back.

Peace.

Gary Gach
March 1997

WHAT
BOOK!?

MITSU SUZUKI

Monastery gate
huge wooden bolt
     fragrant wind

SOYEN SHAKU

En Route to America

Like this boat on this spring ocean
A monk comes or goes by the karma-relation
The horizon seems to be exhaling endlessly
The current, however, takes us to the New World
Yesterday, the whales swam around us.
Today, the clouds shut off the sight of old Japan.
Following the course of Bodhi-Dharma
From the West to the East I go.
Then turning to the South, I may visit
India and Ceylon again, making a pilgrimage like Sudhana
Before long, our boat will enter the Golden Gate
And the sea-gulls, perhaps, may guide me to the destination.

S.S. Cleveland
June 1905

KYOZAN JOSHU

Whenever I hear
the edgeless sound
in the deep night
O Mother!
I find you again.

Whenever I stand beneath the light
of the seamless sky
O Father!
I bow my head.

The sun goes down
Our shadows dissolve

The pine trees darken
O Darling!
We must go home.

DEREK WALCOTT

Love after Love

The time will come
when, with elation,
you will greet yourself arriving
at your own door, in your own mirror,
and each will smile at the other's welcome,

and say, sit here. Eat.
You will love again the stranger who was your self.
Give wine. Give bread. Give back your heart
to itself, to the stranger who has loved you

all your life, whom you ignored
for another, who knows you by heart.
Take down the love letters from the bookshelf,

the photographs, the desperate notes,
peel your own image from the mirror.
Sit. Feast on your life.

NORMAN FISCHER

*Sesshin Poem**

Won't let wanting anything
stand blocking the path –
waiting with alert
anticipation
all day long
in moments
one after the other

Sesshin, literally "to gather the mind," is an intensive period of Zen medita-
tion, usually lasting from five to seven days.

expecting
nothing
determined
never to be disappointed again

A Model of the Universe

What we want is a model of the universe
That includes everything leaving nothing out
Yet is completely different fresh unique holding nothing in
  common
With any of its constituent elements
Yet is not strange exotic and does not make us feel
  uncomfortable
What we want is a model of the universe we can
Read about in a magazine article with pictures
Yet it can't be just another magazine article and it can't
Be in a regular magazine this magazine will glow as it
  shimmers before our eyes
What we want is a model of the universe that will answer all
  our questions
To which we can refer for all sorts of advice
To foretell the future cure bursitis get rich quick aphrodisiac
  etc.
And will be absolutely foolproof one hundred percent of the
  time
What we want is a model of the universe
That we can talk to coyly we can droop our eyelids at
Plump our lower lips begin the sniffle
And it will pat our shoulders say "there there dear" grow
  sad and droopy itself
But without ever really losing its composure or assurance
What we want is a model of the universe so complex we can
  never understand it
So simple we can grasp it in a glance and explain it to our
  friends via a few simple sentences
What we want is a model of the universe
Which once in our possession becomes identified so
  strikingly with us
That we become internationally famous our names
Household words the meaning of our doing and saying

An eternally living legacy around which all subsequent
    culture is organized
What we want is a model of the universe we can count on
    time after time
Yet is never tiring never predictable eternally new
What we want is a model of the universe that is better than
    someone else's model of the universe
That makes their model of the universe look really pale by
    comparison although
Only we realize this we and our intimate friends
But our model of the universe is also better than the
Model of the universe of even our intimate friends
Although the fact of the matter is that no one but us really
Possesses a model of the universe it is our own little secret
However we write poems about it that strike others as
Infinitely suggestive and profound but since this makes us
    feel lonely
We want a model of the universe that everyone understands
We want a model of the universe that explains everything
Yet doesn't take the mystery out of anything in fact adds
    mystery
Even to the simplest of daily actions a model of the universe
    that
Keeps us fit and eating delicate and healthy foods
A model of the universe in which we appear never
    overweight nor old
Yet we don't want to actually appear in this model of the
    universe
We want to be beyond it holding it in our hand looking at it
    from a distance
Yet we don't want to feel alien from it either we want love
We want a model of the universe in which we can always
    stay home
Yet be able to travel whenever we want to remote places
Where all foreign languages are actually English
Though they never lose their ethnic charm
What we want is a model of the universe
Contiguous with the total shape of time
So that it neither begins nor ends is neither something nor
    nothing
What we want is a model of the universe in which
This poem therefore never ends and in which it never began

LAWSON FUSAO INADA

In/Vocation
for Mal Waldron

From the being of me, this
receptacle I am,
I seek and reach
this particular pattern of clouds
clustered on the close horizon,
the ascension of sunlight on the mountains
and the procession therein,

become then, in the sequence,
the presiding precedence of things,
the ordered immediacies,
this graceful grove of trees
meditating
essence of forest
and the slow wind that stirs the sinews,
stimulating the accumulation

of small birds at their calling,
foraging for what abides with winter,
the stuff of what renews
me among grasses and leaves,
the ridges and hollows

of the whole,
entire congregation of collective memory –

choruses, patterns in accordance
with density, intensity,
with destiny –

these sing, these glory, these bring
me pleasure and it spreads through the air
to where you are now,

likewise gifted with gratitude
gracing the brilliant
corners of enclaves
praising rain, this abiding rain
that brings us, takes us, keeps us
huddled in harmonies

now, as deserts, tundras, cities
signal dawn:

Charging, Recharging:
Chanting, Enchanting:

Arise, Arise, Arise, Arise, Arise!

GARY SNYDER

How Poetry Comes to Me

It comes blundering over the
Boulders at night, it stays
Frightened outside the
Range of my campfire
I go to meet it at the
Edge of the light

Song of the Taste

Eating the living germs of grasses
Eating the ova of large birds

  the fleshy sweetness packed
  around the sperm of swaying trees

The muscles of the flanks and thighs of
      soft-voiced cows
    the bounce in the lamb's leap
    the swish in the ox's tail

Eating roots grown swoll
      inside the soil

Drawing on life of living
    clustered points of light spun
      out of space
hidden in the grape.

Eating each other's seed
        eating
    ah, each other.

Kissing the lover in the mouth of bread:
          lip to lip.

Avocado

The Dharma is like an Avocado!
Some parts so ripe you can't believe it,
But it's good.
And other places hard and green
Without much flavor,
Pleasing those who like their eggs well-cooked.

And the skin is thin,
The great big round seed
In the middle,
Is your own Original Nature –
Pure and smooth,
Almost nobody ever splits it open
Or ever tries to see
If it will grow

Hard and slippery,
It looks like
You should plant it – but then
It shoots out thru the
          fingers –
gets away.

Saying Farewell at the Monastery after Hearing the Old Master Lecture on "Return to The Source"

At the last turn in the path
          "goodbye – "
          – bending, bowing,
     (moss and a bit of
          wild
               bird –)
down.

                              Daitoku-ji Monastery

As for Poets

As for poets
The Earth Poets
Who write small poems,
Need help from no man.

■

The Air Poets
Play out the swiftest gales
And sometimes loll in the eddies
Poem after poem,
Curling back on the same thrust.

■

At fifty below
Fuel oil won't flow
And propane stays in the tank.
Fire Poets
Burn at absolute zero
Fossil love pumped back up.

■

The first
Water Poet
Stayed down six years.
He was covered with seaweed.
The life in his poem
Left millions of tiny
Different tracks
Criss-crossing through the mud.

■

With the Sun and Moon
In his belly,
The Space Poet
Sleeps.
No end to the sky –
But his poems,
Like wild geese,
Fly off the edge.

■

A Mind poet
Stays in the house
The house is empty
And it has no walls

The poem
Is seen from all sides,
Everywhere,
At once.

Without

the silence
of nature
within.

the power within.
the power

without.

the path is whatever passes – no
end in itself.

the end is,
grace – ease –

healing,
not saving.

singing
the proof

the proof of the power within.

Earth Verse

Wide enough to keep you looking

Open enough to keep you moving

Dry enough to keep you honest

Prickly enough to make you tough

Green enough to go on living

Old enough to give you dreams

Just Enough

Soil for legs
Axe for hands
Flower for eyes
Bird for ears
Mushroom for nose
Smile for mouth
Songs for lungs
Sweat for skin
Wind for mind

Oshika V, Japan
October 1984

Top Ten of American Poetry

The United States themselves are essentially the greatest
poem. – Walt Whitman

The government of the people, by the people, for the people.
– Thomas Jefferson

You deserve a break today. – McDonald's

Where science gets down to business.
– Rockwell International

Kick the letter habit. – Bell System

Crime hits everybody. Everybody oughta hit back.
– Chicago Crime Commission

Without chemicals life itself would be impossible.
– Monsanto

I think America's future is black, coal black.
– Atlantic Richfield Company

Have a coke and a smile. – Coca Cola

Private property – No trespassing – Dead end road.
– Anonymous

Thanksgiving 1979

If you have time to chatter

Read books

If you have time to read

Walk into mountain, desert and ocean

If you have time to walk

sing songs and dance

If you have time to dance

Sit quietly, you Happy Lucky Idiot

Kyoto
1966

Sugar Loaf Hill

In a beautiful time
There was a shallow sea
With bountiful fish, shells, coral reef and dragon palaces.

Then the sea retreated
And Sugar Loaf was left to rise up on the plain.

Man came to the island and lived in peace quite long.

One day darkness came to the island
With two monstrous armies from north and east
And a crazy war started.

    Thousands of people were killed.
    Thousands of people were wounded.
    Thousands of people became insane.

Finally the war ended
And forty-one years passed like a wind.

Today there are still jet fighters in the sky.
Battle ships in the sea, military tanks on the hills.
How long must we live in such a narrow chasm of war?

    Chilly autumn wind.
    Far away shiny ocean waves, and setting sun.

Here on Sugar Loaf

Where once tremendous blood and tears ran down in the
    war
Now stand side by side
A Buddhist temple and a Catholic church.

        Chilly autumn wind.
        Far away shiny ocean waves, and setting sun.

When I walk down the hill
Where Shakyamuni and Jesus Christ stand side by side
Two little boys shout to me

        "Going home now?"
        "Yes."
        "Let's play together tomorrow!"

Here on Sugar Loaf
Where once tremendous blood and tears ran down in the
    war
Little Shakyamuni and little Jesus Christ shout,

        "let's play together tomorrow!"

November 1986

*(Sugar Loaf is a hill situated in the northeast part of Naha, Okinawa,
fifty meters above sea level. At the end of WWII the battle fought there
cost 2,662 American Marine lives, and left 1,289 insane. The number of
Japanese soldiers and Okinawan civilians killed is unknown.)*

JACK KEROUAC

from *The Scripture of the Golden Eternity*

You are the golden eternity because there is
no me and no you, only one golden eternity.

■

This world is the movie of what everything is,
it is one movie, made of the same stuff
throughout, belonging to nobody, which is what
everything is.

■

Sociability is a big smile, and a big smile is
nothing but teeth. Rest and be kind.

■

The words "atoms of dust" and "the great
universes" are only words. The idea that they
imply is only an idea. The belief that we live here
in this existence, divided into various beings,
passing food in and out of ourselves, and casting off
husks of bodies one after another with no cessation
and no definite or particular discrimination, is
only an idea. The seat of our Immortal Intelligence
can be seen in that beating light between the eyes
the Wisdom Eye of the ancients: we know what
we're doing: we're not disturbed: because
we're like the golden eternity pretending at
playing the magic cardgame and making believe
it's real, it's a big dream, a joyous ecstasy of
words and ideas and flesh, an ethereal flower
unfolding and folding back, a movie, an
exuberant bunch of lines bounding emptiness,
the womb of Avalokitesvara, a vast secret
silence, springtime in the Void, happy young
gods talking and drinking on a cloud. Our
32,000 chillicosms bear all the marks of
excellence. Blind milky light fills our night;
and the morning is a crystal.

■

When you've understood this scripture, throw it
away. If you cant understand this scripture,
throw it away. I insist on your freedom.

■

Kindness and sympathy, understanding and
encouragement, these give: they are better
than just presents and gifts: no reason in the
world why not. Anyhow, be nice. Remember
the golden eternity is yourself. "If someone will
simply practice kindness," said Gotama to
Subhuti, "he will soon attain highest perfect
wisdom." Then he added: "Kindness after all
is only a word and it should be done on the spot
without thought of kindness." By practicing
kindness all over with everyone you will soon
come into the holy trance, definite distinctions
of personalities will become what they really

mysteriously are, our common and eternal blissstuff,
the pureness of everything forever, the great bright
essence of mind, even and one thing everywhere the
holy eternal milky love, the white light everywhere
everything, emptybliss, svaha, shining, ready, and
awake, the compassion in the sound of silence, the
swarming myriad trillionaire you are.

■

Cats yawn because they realize
that there's nothing to do.

■

This world has no marks, signs or evidence of
existence, nor the noises in it, like accident
of wind or voices or heehawing animals,
yet listen closely the eternal hush of silence
goes on and on throughout all this, and has been
going on, and will go on and on. This is because
the world is nothing but a dream and is just thought
of and the everlasting eternity pays no attention
to it. At night under the moon, or in a quiet
room, hush now, the secret music of the Unborn
goes on and on, beyond conception, awake beyond
existence. Properly speaking, awake is not really
awake because the golden eternity never went to
sleep: you can tell by the constant sound of
Silence which cuts through this world like a
magic diamond through the trick of your not
realizing that your mind caused the world.

■

I was smelling flowers in the yard, and when
I stood up I took a deep breath and the blood all
rushed to my brain and I woke up dead on my
back in the grass. I had apparently fainted,
or died, for about sixty seconds. My neighbor
saw me but he thought I had just suddenly
thrown myself on the grass to enjoy the sun.
During that timeless moment of unconsciousness
I saw the golden eternity. I saw heaven. In it
nothing had ever happened, the events of a
million years ago were just as phantom and
ungraspable as the events of now or of a million

years from now, or the events of the next ten
minutes. It was perfect, the golden solitude, the
golden emptiness, Something-Or-Other, something
surely humble. There was a rapturous ring of
silence abiding perfectly. There was no question
of being alive or not being alive, of likes and
dislikes, of near or far, no question of giving
or gratitude, no question of mercy or judgment,
or of suffering or its opposite or anything.
It was the womb itself, aloneness, alaya vijnana
the universal store, the Great Free Treasure, the
Great Victory, infinite completion, the joyful
mysterious essence of Arrangement. It seemed
like one smiling smile, one adorable adoration,
one gracious and adorable charity, everlasting
safety, refreshing afternoon, roses, infinite
brilliant immaterial golden ash, the Golden Age.
The "golden" came from the sun in my eyelids,
and the "eternity" from my sudden instant
realization as I woke up that I had just
been where it all came from and where it
was all returning, the everlasting So, and
so never coming or going; therefore I call it
the golden eternity but you can call it anything
you want. As I regained consciousness I felt so sorry
I had a body and a mind suddenly realizing I
didnt even have a body and a mind and nothing
had ever happened and everything is alright
forever and forever and forever, O thank you
thank you thank you.

Orizaba Blues
  64th Chorus

On the street I seen three guys
standing talking quietly in the sun
and suddenly one guy leaps in pain
and whacks his fingers in the air
as he's burned his hand
    with a match
    lighting a butt

The other two guys dont even
        know this
they go right on talking
        gesticulating with hands

I seen it, it was on San Jose
        Boulevard in St Joseph
        Missouri, nineteen thirty
        two

Them guys didnt even realize
pain is one thing, everywhere?

    Whai? Every golden
    sweetgirl come & befawdle
    her pillow in my hair
        and I dont care?
            Wha?

Written in a tejado rooftop adobe cell
at Orizaba 210, Mexico City, fall 1956
… by candlelight …

Orlanda Blues
24th Chorus

If you once
    for all good
        times
Man's fine
        know
YOU KNOW.

Orlando, Florida
1957

Bath Tub Thought

A rock is like space
because it doesnt move;
And space is like a rock
Because it is empty.
Words are Buddhas.

To Edward Dahlberg

Don't use the telephone.
People are never ready to answer it.
Use poetry.

1970

Haiku

The moon had
    a cat's mustache
For a second.

Missing a kick
    at the icebox door
It closed anyway.

The bottoms of my shoes
    are wet
from walking in the rain.

In my medicine cabinet,
    the winter fly
has died of old age.

Birds singing
    in the dark
– Rainy dawn

ALBERT SAIJO

BODHISATTVA VOWS

BODHISATTVA VOWS TO BE THE LAST ONE OFF
THE SINKING SHIP – YOU SIGN UP & FIND OUT IT'S
FOREVER –   PASSENGER LIST ENDLESS – SHIP

NEVER EMPTIES – SHIP KEEPS SINKING BUT DOESN'T GO QUITE UNDER – ON BOARD ANGST PANIC & DESPERATION HOLD SWAY – TURNS OUT BODHISATTVAHOOD IS A FUCKING JOB LIKE ANY OTHER BUT DIFFERENT IN THAT THERE'S NO WEEKENDS HOLIDAYS VACATIONS NO GOLDEN YEARS OF RETIREMENT – YOU'RE SPENDING ALL YOUR TIME & ENERGY GETTING OTHER PEOPLE OFF THE SINKING SHIP INTO LIFEBOATS BOUND GAILY FOR NIRVANA WHILE THERE YOU ARE SINKING – & OF COURSE YOU HAD TO GO & GIVE YOUR LIFEJACKET AWAY – SO NOW LET US BE CHEERFUL AS WE SINK – OUR SPIRIT EVER BUOYANT AS WE SINK.

BOB KAUFMAN

… solitary thoughts on death and other illegal mysteries carried off in the hurricane afternoon's warped glimpse of buried events squeezed from pits of stagnant wax ripped from walls of the mind's eye of goethe taking faust by the hand across dark teutonic landscapes … to tuscan dusky twilights where torchlit italians carved life in marble mountains ankle-deep in severed heads of bloody popes at war with god for rome's remains only to settle for splendored tombs sprung from hands of deathless spirits in tunics of blood and dust crouched in corners of light where creation is master and man does not exist except as tools of art …

from Does the Secret Mind Whisper?

THE TRIP, DHARMA TRIP, SANGHA TRIP
IS A DELIBERATE ATTEMPT TO
REBUILD A LIFE, SEEMS TO
BE DEMOLISHED LIKE AN OLD
BUILDING NOBODY WANTS TO
LIVE IN YET STANDS HOPEFULLY.
SOMETHING MORE THAN MEMORY IS

NEEDED, WORDS ARE NOT A SOLUTION,
SOMETIMES THEY ARE A PROBLEM.
BUT THE PEAK MUST BE REACHED;
THE ROAD GOES ONLY TO THE
TOP OF THE MOUNTAIN, SEEMS
THERE IS NO PLACE ELSE TO GO,
LIFE ON A MOUNTAIN TOP WITH
SKY ALL AROUND, A VIEW OF
EVERYTHING SPREADING OUT
BEFORE THE EYES, REPLACING
WORDS WITH IMAGES.

Final journal entry
1985

AL YOUNG

Third Street Promenade;
Full Moon, Sunday Night, Santa Monica

The hands of the clock have stayed still
at half past eleven for fifty years.
It is always opening time in the Sailors Arms.
– Dylan Thomas
Under Milk Wood

The Buddhist approach to packing up after the gig
requires no time; it unfolds moment by moment –
a dirty shirt here, a lost button there, all the slips
of paper, cassettes and more cassettes, wet socks
wrung out and bagged in zipper-snagged plastic,
badly slowing slips of mind concentrated like sunlight.
Starlight is what we're made of, is how we function clearly.
There is no other way to get right down to the history
of getting out of town. Uncrowded increments of space
make possible the way time works, the way it plays.
The big, slick moon, the ocean, palms, the high-rise
film-set backdrop of this misty physical night, set in desert,
done up green and brown, and grandly watered; understood.
While joggers and power-walkers line and fill Ocean Avenue's
manicured edges, plentifully, clinically, oxygen must fend
for itself. Air, like love, lies largely where you find it.

Here in the sixth largest nation on earth, where dreaming
is an industry, where belief is everything, and sunshine God,
the century ends. Transition seems everything, content
gridlock; this life, this style of going away and coming back.
The drawbacks, come-ons, exquisite alibis and raps this road
life requires get matched and met by always coming home.
And where is home? The present moment, right now, wherever
travelers find themselves. Not only is home pre-sent; it's postpaid,
upgraded every moment, constructed of breathing-room and
nothingness: the perfect relaxation tool for any foolish voyageur.
Just as time unpacks itself and readies balanced, opened minds
– for sudden shifts in plans, a change of heart, dramatic drops,
earthquakes, the shutting down of freeways, re-routed baggage,
roots – so you book and pack again for the only place you know.

PHILIP WHALEN

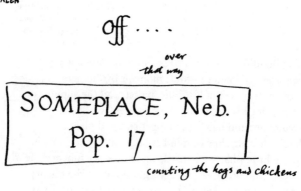

Take dandelions first salad, { THIS IS NOT AN EXAMPLE, I MEAN look ~ }
    then yellow flower,

maybe chains of them — kids pick them ~~~~~ delicate faceted sphere gray white sphere

gray haired overnight (or day) .

                    completion, fruition, what you will

        delicately faceted sphere GONE !
            (as a sensible structure) .
                            where am I ?

    what is it
        I'm doing ?

                    you Imagine that I'm ignoring you
                    or trying to humiliate

        The moral { most restrictively }   on the one hand, discontinued
once it was less so → THE DANDELION <
sometime it might   on the other, grows wings ?
be otherwise

                    I never said you had to Do
                        anything about it or
                        change your life in any respect

    I only forbid you to draw any false
            analogies
                what's the coat on the chair
                    before you think of its name ?

ABSOLUTE

REALITY, namely,
how much can I do right now
about life in this place ? I
am it, all of this living
AND this place and what
I'm doing is called

TRANSFORMATION
    IRRADIATION

BASE METAL BECOMES

    GOLD

Tuesday July 25, 1961

hoist great blocks of language into place
A fabric of elegant proportion, exquisitely adorned
with garlands, columns, urns
one chaste Roman statue in a niche

Wherein the lives & feelings of a motley crew sparkle,
flare, shout, gasp & tinkle,

ancient gaudy jeweled king=
doms of the east..!

Disperse into foreign cities

Ah, the dream of several seconds, that are centuries
I pass through Max Bruch forest, dallying on my way towards
the pinnace in the wooded bay
the final Journey to Cythera

⊡

15·XII·66

PET SHOP

DEAD BIRDS

AND LIVE ONES
LOCKED IN THE SAME
CAGE AGAINST THE
WINDOW

The End of the line.

Carefully try to remember what
it is that you are doing. "How
do you do? How do you like
what you do?" are you going
to continue in the same wasteful
and thoughtless fashion   ?

21 V 64
Philip Whalen

Nasturtiums
22 V 64

SATURDAY

Tough
New
            grass & weeds
Replace mud
            beer cans & scraps of paper
Green thick & rough
Surrounded by cement

        While from every window
        Of a tiny station wagon
        A great solemn dog looks out
                (not hanging head over,
                    tongue flopping)
        Sitting upright, calm as bears, the
Ancient hippy long grey hair driving,
Young chick beside him, all excited
            Yakking

                            Philip Whalen
                            16: III : 75

JOANNE KYGER

Never talk ahead
            of time
            about
        what isn't.
                    This is living
                            to give you a present

Duncan's class met last night and more talk
about vowels and consonants – the boredom of it to
me relieved only by the fact that Robert arrived
quite high on martinis. Afterwards, Spicer, Duncan,
Ebbe, George Stanley, Joe Dunn & I walked thru the
Broadway tunnel to The Place – Spicer on the Anti-
Beatnik Book of the Month Club side, and Joe, Robert
Duncan and I forming a new faction – The Dharma
Committee.

from journal
October 9, 1958

It's a great day. Last night I visited my old
childhood town of Lake Bluff, Illinois. The
Creeleys and Philip Whalen were there. I took
a walk to Lake Michigan with Philip to see it all
built up in the form of a great amusement center.
Lost in its intricacies I go to work. Stepping out
a door I land in a great field and run a tractor up
and down the rows, not exactly enough, to be sure
and run back into the amusement center, donning my
waitress uniform on the way, before I get caught,
before I get caught. Oh Ladies of the Middle West,
how do your hands get rough. What is this self
I think I will lose if I leave what I know. Back
to the dark bedroom and aimless unhappy adolescent
lives. Lacking any commitment to the actual living
ground, life becomes pointless in its urge of culture,
quote unquote, Art. There, I've said it, in all its
simpleness – the best teacher lives outside, the best
teacher lives inside you, beating blood, breathing
air, the best teacher is alive.

Bird family
boat going out to sea
all this
every day

Dream

I'm doing this poetry reading with Simone
and I have nothing ready to read but the funny papers.
So I make up a poem about the

     GOLD   LIGHT   BUDDHA
It has a sappy ending. There is no audience
response. The LIGHTS aren't even on.

Kwan Yin means a Person
who *sees* the *sounds* of the world
And perceives the cries of people
in distress

                    She can manifest herself
at will
       to help those mortals.

So Please   Bring me the Light!

"Oh Man is the highest type of animal existing
    or known to have existed
        but differs from other animals
       more in his extraordinary mental
    development than in anatomical
structure ..."
                Well when I think of men
      I think of them in a sexual manner
Otherwise, I don't notice the difference, you know

being absorbed as *being*   one just thinks 'people'
and not 'male' and 'female' so much as someone
to *talk* to.   And how men are all

the same being born from Man and Woman and out
    of a woman's body commonly known as 'Mother'.
"And God said let us make MAN in our own image,
    after our likeness and let them have dominion."

     And "Nature may stand up
          and say to all the world,
              'This was a MAN!'"
    And then "I pronounce you MAN

and wife."

                    Daddy you is dandy
when you're here.   Shrill and soft old Autumnal
            winds blow   and we are tucked below
the shallow soil where seeds spring
                              up and wither quickly
            flirting madly.

                    I've got him now,
        the beautiful one for my part
of the year here in my dark

            and expensive underground
        all mine before he is shared
and killed again by the fearless boar
            he is hunting and torn apart
and his blood runs out and red roses and anemones
bloom   and it is spring   and
                        he is gone again
That man about town gone again ...

The Empty Shrine Buddha

If you grow your hair you save on heating bills
Thus the globe rolls over

                        Poverty is something
Money can't buy.

                                    Summer 1987

PATRICIA DONEGAN

Something Happened
   October 1986, Kyoto, Japan

Awakened at 3 a.m.
I go down to the outhouse
absolute stillness, all asleep
over the Kyoto hills

no bell from Kurodani temple
imperceptible wind blowing
between bright stars
red maples barely moving
my faint breath in & out
is this how the centuries pass unnoticed?

Something happened somewhere
did my mother die
was there an earthquake in Tokyo
is my lover making love with another
was a Buddha born
did a leaf drop from this tree?

Half-Open

These days
I wear my robe half-open
the purple silk parts, showing scarlet lining
the thick blue sash, a tangle on the floor,
I sway around the house easily
feel the weight of the robe
a cool breeze on my skin as I pass the window
& see no one's watching
only blue sky outlines clear-cut mountains half-clothed
& green grass tufts peek through
the cracked brown earth.

Tonight
while shampooing my hair
for the first time
I felt my skull.

from Bone Poems

ANDREW SCHELLING

Run My Hand Under

> *Does Nature remember, think you, that they were men,*
> *or not rather that they are bones?*
> *– H. D. Thoreau*

In a redwood grove, on a low hill facing east, I bent over a shovel and buried my dog. Sun pierces a tree, the far ridge, a fresh growth already laces the turned-over sod. St. John's wort in the shade. Where dirt's most disturbed poison oak. Oneself, to end up, on a coastal North American hill, somewhere, hell realm or bardo, beyond whatever – a comfort to consider those bones –

Or run my hand over elastic frail ribcage, the woman I love, her pulse of desire. What store of affection inside the bonehouse? Tilt of the chin, and how her denim skirt falls to her shoes. The things a man loves. Her face could be face of a dog. Face of ash. Ash and a trickle of bone.

It's an old Buddhist trick, got out of Mongolia, some paleolithic recess up north. Dress up in fur. Take off the fur. See your companion a scatter of bone. Two ossuaries, just a membrane between you. Remove it like clothes.

Now love her like that. Take off her fur.

Taste a nipple, go for rough skin but find rib. Thigh against thigh, seeming so fierce, it's only a femur, good for a flute. Try to be delicate, back on your passion, tangle of nerve and wet tissue, all those veins at the crotch. Find pelvis – hollow and dry. I came through that? Hard cartilage. Now try her mouth and touch teeth.

Knucklebone, bone of the ankle, down past the kneecap. Run my hand under, beneath beneath. Where does it come from? How did it get here?

Yet it's heaped on the bed. Next to a window. Imagine the aftermath. Hipbone on hip.

September 1986

ANNE WALDMAN

Yum Yab

How many heads,
wily, cynical do I have?
How many snakes hiss forth this skull
How many arms to clasp the lover
who trembles, shudders
in multiple embrace
How many adornments,
weapons, power implements, planets
are wielded thus, thrust about,
spinning their whizz and gleam
How much spittle, menses,
blood, lymph,
tears, urine
does it take to turn it around
How many pores on how many breasts
arms & legs
Exits, entrances to carry you through
How many mouths
to speak your name = Deity Masculine =
& you return in another form, purified
lopped off, never emasculated
diminished of arrogance
liberated from an old karmic push
Master of the Universe
released to become subservient
before we become equals
& you will play the other side, try it
you will be objectified in my lists & games
Together we ride
Together we ride
& you will be my gratified desire
Enter the gate –
gate of cervix,
How you are finally my doll
my puppet, lost brother
my split-off side
processed, shaped by largesse, by rage
by bondage

How many times I ask for retribution,
ask you be placed here
astride my body
as consort, as adornment
as lateral mind
as thinking into absolutes
not a chance encounter
no histories of the men loom here
Erase the obvious ones
who seek dominion
who plundered the womb
who would only conquer what they fear
Turn in around
Retrace the steps
Back, back
uncover the ancestor
Recalcitrant one
Who bore you first?
This rocks the plan, this is the
first spark
latitudinous
unrehearsed
a broken form
Picture a monument
a state of mind
a lowing beast, a head held high
a last resort, a lay public
a hieratic thrust, a witness to
exploits monetary, & sexual
a scowl, a forehead that
looks as if thinking
that blazes its many fiery tongues
a tonsure, hope's envy
to be fortified by night
to be exquisitely decked out by day
naked, absolute, over a fine edge,
sleep ridden, driven by dream,
power is not her metaphor
longed for, divided
lusty, estranged from her shore
languishing for cities

lusting for completion
divided against herself
and needing you, ornament,
my subjugated "other"

RICK FIELDS

The Very Short Sutra on
the Meeting of the Buddha and the Goddess

Thus have I made up:
    Once the Buddha was walking
    along the forest path in the Oak Grove at Ojai,
    walking without arriving anywhere or having any
    thought of arriving or not arriving.
And lotuses, shining with the morning dew
    miraculously appeared under every step
    Soft as silk beneath the toes of the Buddha.
When suddenly, out of the turquoise sky,
    dancing in front of his half-shut inward-looking
    eyes, shimmering like a rainbow
    or a spider's web
    transparent as the dew on a lotus flower
    – the Goddess appeared quivering
    like a hummingbird in the air before him.
She, for she was surely a she
    as the Buddha could clearly see
    with his eye of discriminating awareness wisdom,
was mostly red in color
    though when the light shifted
    she flashed like a rainbow.
She was naked except
    for the usual flower ornaments
    goddesses wear.
    Her long hair
    was deep blue, her eyes fathomless pits
    of space, and her third eye a bloodshot
    song of fire.
The Buddha folded his hands together
    and greeted the Goddess thus:

"O goddess, why are you blocking my path?
     Before I saw you I was happily going nowhere.
     Now I'm not so sure where I go."
"You can go around me,"
     said the Goddess, twirling on her heel like a bird
     darting away,
     but just a little way away,
     "or you can come after me
     but you can't pretend I'm not here,
     This is my forest, too."
With that the Buddha sat
     supple as a snake
     solid as a rock
     beneath a Bo tree
     that sprang full-leaved
     to shade him.
"Perhaps we should have a chat,"
     he said.
     "After years of arduous practice
     at the time of the morning star
     I penetrated reality and ..."
"Not so fast, Buddha," the Goddess said,
     "I am reality."

     The earth stood still,
     the oceans paused,
     the wind itself listened
     – a thousand arhats, bodhisattvas and dakinis
     magically appeared to hear
     what would happen in the conversation.
"I know I take my life in my hands,"
     said the Buddha,
     "But I am known as the Fearless One
     – so here goes."
And he and the Goddess
     without further words
     exchanged glances.
Light rays like sun beams
     shot forth
     so brightly that even
     Sariputra, the All-Seeing One,
     had to turn away.

And then they exchanged thoughts
And the illumination was as bright as a diamond candle
And then they exchanged minds
And there was a great silence as vast as the universe that
    contains everything
And then they exchanged bodies
And then clothes
And the Buddha arose
    as the Goddess
    and the Goddess arose as the Buddha.
And so on back and forth
    for a hundred thousand hundred thousand kalpas.
If you meet the Buddha
    you meet the Goddess.
    If you meet the Goddess,
    you meet the Buddha.
Not only that. This:
    The Buddha is emptiness,
    The Goddess is bliss.
    The Goddess is emptiness,
    The Buddha is bliss.
    And that is what
    And what-not you are
    It's true.
So here comes the mantra of the Goddess and the Buddha,
the unsurpassed non-dual mantra. Just to say this mantra,
just to hear this mantra once, just to hear one word of this
mantra once makes everything the way it truly is: OK.
So here it is:
    Earth-walker / sky-walker
    Hey silent one, Hey great talker
    Not two / not one
    Not separate / not apart
    This is the heart
    Bliss is emptiness
    Emptiness is bliss
    Be your breath, Ah
    Smile, Hey, And relax, Ho
    Remember: You can't miss.

Ojai Foundation, Ojai, California
"Engaging American Buddhism" retreat for artists
with Thich Nhat Hanh
May 1987

STEVE SANFIELD

Alone in the house
Springtime snow
You everywhere

GARY ROSENTHAL

Wild Hooves

The love poems
I want to write
had not been lived ...

Embarrassed, I now want
to burn,
sweep,
erase
all evidence
of how I've loved before ...

And the crust
that had covered
my heart?

trampled
by wild hooves
of your beauty

GILLIAN COOTE

You

I know all the notes of your voice
all the cat-fox eye glints
and grey sheen cheeks.
I know your face.

I know
all the strength and
power of your heart

and the charged space around
your being.

I know
the spring that's tripped
in me
my hair-breadth heart that
plunges and swoops,
a lion-kite on a
wild journey.

JANE HIRSHFIELD

The Adamantine Perfection of Desire

Nothing more strong
than to be helpless before desire.

No reason,
the simplified heart whispers,
the argument over,
only This.

No longer choosing anything but assent.

Its bowl scraped clean to the bottom,
the skull-bone cup no longer horrifies,
but, rimmed in silver, shines.

A spotted dog follows a bitch in heat.
Gray geese fly past us, crying.
The living cannot help but love the world.

MITSU SUZUKI

Swiftly walking away
someone set a lamp
in the darkness
under the tree

JAAN KAPLINSKI

Once I got a postcard from the Fiji Islands
with a picture of sugar cane harvest. Then I realized
that nothing at all is exotic in itself.
There is no difference between digging potatoes in our
    Mutiku garden
and sugar cane harvesting in Viti Levu.
Everything that is is very ordinary
or, rather, neither ordinary nor strange.
Far-off lands and foreign peoples are a dream,
a dreaming with open eyes
somebody does not wake from.
It's the same with poetry – seen from afar
it's something special, mysterious, festive.
No, poetry is even less
special than a sugar cane plantation or potato field.
Poetry is like sawdust coming from under the saw
or soft yellowish shavings from a plane.
Poetry is washing hands in the evening
or a clean handkerchief that my late aunt
never forgot to put in my pocket.

MAXINE HONG KINGSTON

25 December

<u>Write</u> before other people get up. Dress.
Let the other people have at the day.
Stay conscious. Give them insurance
to ink. Afternoon – write when they leave.
Go to Carmen's house, see Joseph.
Evening before bed – <u>write</u>.

26 Dec.

An idea – that the process is
best when easy. "Calm. Ease."
Drive to Berkeley. Call John.
Dinner out – S.F.? –
And the way to control anything
is to be aware of it.

Thursday

Today, woke up remembering
and looking ahead. Tried to
focus by meditation.
Then made alarm go
off in pool house – the
alarm had gone off
at 3:50 or so, and I
went out to fix it –
Earl turned on the
news, made him stop –
postum and wrote (an
idea came during
meditation) – now I'll
have breakfast, write,
make the bed, dress.
At 9:00 or so – make calls –
the architect, check list
of calls. Write some more.
Maybe shower at Bessie's.
Invite her to dinner at
Faculty Club? Is there
anything I need at her
house? The mail &
calls. <u>In the American
Grain</u>. School – go a
little early – apptmts.
Dinner. Work on
writing, letters,
insurance.
Saturday – Began w/ meditation
Write. Decide whether to go to
the framers. Letters to Nikki
Giovanni, Mary Gordon,
Toni Morrison.

February 20, 1992

Very upset on verge of cold
& coffee. Today, concentrate
on one thing at a time –
you don't have to say or
do everything. Write –

then collect things for Bessie's
house. Check on plane
tickets. Have grapefruit.
Picture for Cal Book –
School. Go to 35 up
movie? Get some
black ink.

26 May
Today – plan the future – Phone
Jeannine to add another day.
Phone New York & change
the film date. Phone
Krueger to talk about the
plans. Go to school, shop
for the bed.
4:15 p.m. woke up from nap – earlier – bought
bed, called Krueger's & Joseph –
some writing – grades _in._

■

This afternoon, do some writing,
clean the house. School
_is_ over – nice talking w/
Larry to end it – 3 months
before school starts.

Do some writing. Organize house.
Maybe finish the insurance.

■

Forgot the mail. Forgot to
do banking

27 May
        Not bad meditation –
normal, sweet – water
plants –
Last night's dream –
        ladders take us to
heaven & other side
of darkness & bottom
of planet – it will
be a long time before
my father & I will

be together again.
The ladders up to
Mom's house / bedroom
where if we put food
the birds come, &
the animals are
from Pop's world.
Mom says don't feed
them & let them in the house.

■

Suddenly free from the life
that my parents had me
for the purpose of torturing
me.

How did I become convinced
of such craziness?

And how did I get free?

■

Thought about 3:15 a.m. Oct. 27, 1992
written afternoon next day –
in the Japanese room

The street corner orderly
the lines, trees as is –
just right.

The dawn took forever
until I learned it
was the middle of the night

and I was wide-awake
jet-lagged

Dark with <u>streetlights</u> –
still – no traffic and
no people

Respite – the exact
present moment

The way the light <u>falls</u>
is perfect

from journals

GARRETT HONGO

Something Whispered in the **Shakuhachi**

No one knew the secret of my flutes,
and I laugh now
because some said
I was enlightened.
But the truth is
I'm only a gardener
who before the War
was a dirt farmer and learned
how to grow the bamboo
in ditches next to the fields,
how to leave things alone
and let the silt build up
until it was deep enough to stink
bad as night soil, bad
as the long, witch-grey
hair of a ghost.

No secret in that.

My land was no good, rocky,
and so dry I had to sneak
water from the whites,
hacksaw the locks off the chutes at night,
and blame Mexicans, Filipinos,
or else some wicked spirit
of a migrant, murdered in his sleep
by sheriffs and wanting revenge.
Even though they never believed me,
it didn't matter – no witnesses,
and my land was never thick with rice,
only the bamboo
growing lush as old melodies
and whispering like brush strokes
against the fine scroll of wind.

I found some string in the shed
or else took a few stalks
and stripped off their skins,
wove the fibers, the floss,

into cords I could bind
around the feet, ankles, and throats
of only the best bamboos.
I used an ice pick for an awl,
a fish knife to carve finger holes,
and a scythe to shape the mouthpiece.

I had my flutes.

▪

When the War came,
I told myself I lost nothing.

My land, which was barren,
was not actually mine but leased
(we could not own property)
and the shacks didn't matter.

What did were the power lines nearby
and that sabotage was suspected.

What mattered to me
were the flutes I burned
in a small fire
by the bath house.

▪

All through Relocation,
in the desert where they put us,
at night when the stars talked
and the sky came down
and drummed against the mesas,
I could hear my flutes
wail like fists of wind
whistling through the barracks.
I came out of Camp,
a blanket slung over my shoulder,
found land next to this swamp,
planted strawberries and beanplants,
planted the dwarf pines and tended them,
got rich enough to quit
and leave things alone,
let the ditches clog with silt again
and the bamboo grow thick as history

So, when it's bad now,
when I can't remember what's lost
and all I have for the world to take
means nothing,
I go out back of the greenhouse
at the far end of my land
where the grasses go wild
and the arroyos come up
with cat's-claw and giant dahlias,
where the children of my neighbors
consult with the wise heads
of sunflowers, huge against the sky,
where the rivers of weather
and the charred ghosts of old melodies
converge to flood my land
and sustain the one thicket
of memory that calls for me
to come and sit
among the tall canes
and shape full-throated songs
out of wind, out of bamboo,
out of a voice
that only whispers.

ALAN CHONG LAU

wintermelon

inside each one
hides a snowflake
woven by a spider

bittermelon

i like mine overripe

seeds the color of blood
gleam in collapsing ridges
of wet yellow flesh

eating habits of the old man
for yasunari kawabata, in beauty and sadness

when i lost my teeth
all of them
i couldn't eat loquats
the way i used to
in one, two bites

now i glide them against
the soft of my mouth
a pink ridge wrinkled to a smooth roughness
like the insides of a pickled oyster

the membrane of the fruit
in a soft crush
juice sucked clean by a regular puckering
the lips almost swallow back mouth

when i am through
with the meat of the loquat
i kick the pit out
with the tip of my tongue

my wife won't eat
at the same table
with me and my loquats
but then we never did get along very well

i have always loved loquats
and now without teeth
well, the pleasure is double

morning reflections over the miso soup
for kazuko

the silence of knife
flat on cutting board
speaks to me of morning

mottled leaves
fat robins finishing off berries
the dog who won't leave the door

spears of scallions

sprinkled atop the steam of miso
bobbing green boats
in a hot brown sea

my wife wants to know
what time it is

RUSSELL LEONG

What Does the Body Dream at Rest?

If the heat of one body resting
Equals seventy lotus flowers
What does the body dream at rest?

The boy fell into the sea and it swept him away
Said those who watched him tumble off the cliff;
Of course, they could not feel what he felt
As his legs, like scissors, cut the waves.

The boy entered the green fold of the sea
As water raced up his heels and thighs
Bared his belly and chest
Salted his lips and tongue.
So he sank beyond the gaze of those
Who stood panicked against the sky
Shuffling pebbles at their feet.

Divers dove into the surf
And later rose to bring the body back
To where the mother and father
Waiting on the boat
Began to rub his hands and feet
To render him alive again.
But his eyes stared at the empty sky
So they closed his lids and wailed a while
Before they tossed carnations into the sea.

The father, despite his firm belief
Felt his son was lost to him forever
So he fingered his rosary beads
A hundred-and-eight times

As he cried out for his breath.
The mother promised herself
She'd watch him forty days-and-nine
And pray to the guardian of Hell
To reject her son from his realm.
She'd wait for words to part his lips
She too wanted to slip into the sea
But she dropped incense into the waves instead
Where they dipped and flickered like fireflies.

My place is where souls do not cry anymore –
I am sincerely sorry, said the man at the morgue;
We'll drain the blood and embalm him neatly
You won't see any holes or cuts.
But this is against our beliefs, they said.
Why this is L.A., said the man, I've worked with Mexicans
And Muslims, Jews and Jehovahs,
Blacks and Buddhists –
And never run into folks like you before!

My son is suspended in space, she said
In another state of grace, said he
Thus he may come back to us
But without blood he has no chance to live
So we'll stay here and chant for him by turns.
But if we don't drain the blood, said the man
The boy will rot for sure.
Then we'll freeze him, the father said
And we'll pay you to keep his body whole
For forty days-and-nine; for on the final day
Unthaw him; if he doesn't resurrect
Then burn his body, return the ashes to me.

Am I only dreaming of his breath? asked the father
My boy is dreaming of his birthday, said the mother
Next month he will turn eighteen, she reminded him
Who nodded silently and began to wring
His hands this way and that.

After the boy passed into the sea
His breath passed simply through his bones
Darkness, then dawn came and left him
Drifting off the coast of Calafia –

Palos Verdes, Catalina, Baja, Mexico
Away from the lonely continent he lived.

Then the evening star and burning ray
Arose and revealed to him in turn
That what was love, or lost
Was the same at the heart of the sutra –
"In the void there are no forms,
No feelings, ideas, impulses, consciousness
No eye, ear, nose, tongue, body or mind …"

If the heat of one body resting
Equals seventy lotus flowers
What does the body dream at rest?

January 4, 1997

Threads

There is no way to show it.
No way to even break it or
Burn it or throw it away.
It is with me. And yet
There is nothing I can say
And nothing I can do
That will make it work.

It is with me.
A fish swimming in silence.
A fruit ripening on a tree.
A bulging in the back of my mind
Like a fat insect caught on threads.

PAULA YUP

The Things I Miss

Making love in the Painted Desert.
Pachinko parlors in Shinjuku.
Dim sum in Vancouver's Chinatown.
My mother's shark fin soup in Phoenix, Arizona.
A green flash sunset at Wood Neck Beach.

Peking duck in the New Territories.
So many bicycles on Ghanzhou streets.
Hot Phoenix sidewalks burning my bare feet.
Saunas and the bathhouse with my friend Mariko.
Going to the Mao bookstore in Tokyo,
and Maashiko pottery stores with another friend.
Tokyo hotel rooms with my Japanese lover.
Tokyo Tower, St. Alban's Church and the Soviet Embassy.
The pastel buildings of Macau, the dog races
and the casino with robbing one-armed bandits.
Making love in Beebe Woods on Cape Cod.
The ferry from Woods Hole to Martha's Vineyard.
Catching fireflies into jars on School St. in Woods Hole.
My Mexican babysitter's homemade hot sauce
and the piñata party she gave
when I tried to hit a piñata with a stick
and didn't get any candy which made me sad.
My Mexican babysitter making homemade flour tortillas.
Getting an all-body tan on Wreck Beach in Vancouver.
Emily Carr's paintings at the Vancouver Art Gallery.
The streets of Granville Island.
Doing zazen with a friend in Okurayama.
Looking at five hundred pictures of China
in an Okurayama park with another friend.
My grandfather's mansion in Hong Kong
which I never saw. My grandfather in Hong Kong
who I never met and whose funeral I didn't go to.
Making love at the beach on Big Sycamore Canyon.
A student's party in Tokyo at his grandfather's house
where I saw a priceless painting of cherry blossoms
and the grandfather's priceless and very old bonsai tree.
The hydrofoil from Kowloon to Macau.
Translating Japanese poems into English in jazz coffee shops.
Kawabata's house in Kamakura with his things still there.
My teacher Mori Joji, the grandson of Mori Ogai
(the Shakespeare of Japan), who taught the only class I loved
at Waseda University.
The bamboo poles the Japanese hang their clothes on
to air dry in the busy breezes.
Sushi, sashimi, soba and sake for eating and drinking.

Plum wine on special days.
Taking a walk with a Finnish friend
and seeing a spiderweb with dew like beads on it
on a trip to Mt. Fuji and Hakone
and almost missing the bus back.
Eating a chrysanthemum in a Tokyo restaurant
because a friend said they did so in Japan,
and I'll never forget the bitter taste
or the smile on my friend's face.

TELLY WONG

Loneliness

A voice
On the phone
Without face
Without form
The waiting
The call
The one hour
When we are together
Poetry in the dark
The one hour
The call
The waiting.

MITSU SUZUKI

Summer butterfly
  one-meeting one-lifetime
deep valley

WILLIAM R. LAFLEUR

Wedding Party

a flow of champagne
and of monks moving through
the crowd with bowls
and silverware: a pile
of shoes at the threshold
as the people inside get
more dense, more liquid,
more ready to dance;
the tall bride's family members
wear flowers and shoes
and happily
stand out even here where
in all ten directions there
is nothing
but crowd

STEVE SANFIELD

Birthday Poem

Inside – the laughter of friends.
Outside – the moon & I alone.

JUDYTH COLLIN

The Layman's Lament

Shame on you Shakyamuni for setting
the precedent
of leaving home.
Did you think it was not there –
    in your wife's lovely face
    or your baby's laughter?
Did you think you had to go   elsewhere
to find it?

Tsk, tsk.
I am here to show you
dear sir
that you needn't step
even one sixteenth of an inch away – stay
here – elbows dripping with soapy water
        stay   here – spit up all over your chest
           stay here – steam rising in lazy curls from
                                cream of wheat
Poor Shakyamuni – sitting under that Bo tree
                           miles away from home
Venus shone all the while

JOHN TARRANT

Han Shan in Santa Rosa

She walks down the hall carrying
her doll, the present widens
and she is the first treasure and the last,
not as the trees are,
mossed with winter rains,
not as my enemy is
who leads me secret alleys
into tranquility, and not
as dolphin, field or star,
but in a sweet intensity of heart
more personal than I thought
my heart could bear
in outward voyage.
She has and is a light which is
to feed her, clean her, hide and seek
and swings and books,
so she has joined us to the world
and to each other
in a density that, fragile, seems
beyond unjoining.
In this garden we suffer and become
our own work.
I became her left hand and her right.

Fog enters from the Pacific.
The trees are near.
I can't remember the road I came on.

CAITLIN O'DONNELL

Footprints

Which way are you going?
Footprints   footprints
Outside the window
Little dancing footprints
My heart is doing treesongs

ALEX MARLOWE

He Does Not Give the Reader One Line of Information

The dragon
of chaos proceeds
finding gold earth
stars. Alchemical
bottles of Guinness
Stout sprout
eating chocolate
fish under
the soothing
moon and astronauts

JESSEMYN MEYERHOFF

snow

In the morning
when I wake in the cocoon of my dreams
all silence has been restored

all silence so persuasive as to hang on the trees, to bend
   them
to the ground,
to snuff out the flower's burning bright petals,
to *shhhh* the soft buddha statue on the walk way.
I open my eyes;
I rip my cocoon from my sides, my sticky, fragile wings
and fly into this morning of snow.

the resounding echo of the buddha's words

from the old memories, the web that swims under the waves
and the pulsing of the tides
and over the land,
that thrives in the wind.
From the extragalactic memories that harbor aureoles of
white light,
comes one,
swiftly rushing, heavily laden sound
      that I have heard before
      that I will hear again
                        and again
in my mind, until it dies away in the dusk, settles into the
   shadows.
The sound, descending, broken by nothing in its
      circling breath.
            The gong of a bell.

a million times

A man comes to the door (a million times)
and says he wants to be a monk.
He sits and stares
on his own appointed cushion at his own appointed piece of
   wall.
Or at his shadow,
the way it flickers and moves in the morning.
Or at his hands with his two thumbs pressed tightly together
   to keep them from curling away,
sinking into the groove where his ankles meet.

Or at his neighbor, out of the corner of his eye,
the way his neighbor sags forward and drops his head.
He reminds himself to be mindful (a million times)
and when I meet him on the path he always bows to me,
    quietly,
and asks me how my day has been and am I shining
    grandly?
I have seldom met a monk and daily meet a buddha,
a child or a mother or a whale in song.

NOVA RAY

The Last Flower

Every day I create for you
a little bit more of nothing.
The Buddha says, "The north cannot be
without the south."
But I am in the east ...
and you in the west.
You have eaten the apple
of good and evil
finding me in the wrong.
And I have become
your disappointment.
Her water turns to glass.
Y nuestras vidas son rios
que van a dar en el mar.
The Buddha says, "The north cannot be
without the south."
But I am in the east ...
and you in the west.

JAMIE MEYERHOFF

On Impermanence

Rose-blushing   heaven-scented pear ("that pear's a

bite of sunlight")
set to glow in perfect ripeness and beauty on my dresser
    softening to brown mush, released to the soil and sun.
We walk through the forest and you
exclaim at wildflowers, the green unfurling leaves of the
  maples
shot through with life.
Should I say aloud – everywhere, I see decay
the fallen bodies of trees
layers of wood   vegetation   mulch   emptying into dark
  soil.
We stand
surrounded by death.

Three Ravens

She was sitting at her window
    looking at the dusty road and dripping
        trees   moss on trunks and fallen leaves
   when
life came through.
Their wings swept out the beat of time
        the throb of the heart and intake of breath.
Their wings were blacker than nothingness
    their goal was fixed; their minds
were emptiness
    They landed among the dry dead leaves
    of sycamores
and the world   fell apart in beauty.

ALLISON HARRIS

Nothing Much

Nothing much just ...
A burst of light on the horizon
A flash of blue light over in dusty sky
A lone stone being stroked by whipping waves
A triumphant blow of a golden horn

A speck of sand named "Harry" on the glittering
banks
A sweet taste of peppermint tea
A whiff of old picture books
A muddy puddle knee high
A screech of chalk on a chalk board
An old homework assignment crumpled
A marshmallow squishing under feet
An old painting hanging crookedly
Nothing much at all

WILL STAPLE

Shen Tao

Shen Tao was not afraid
        because he didn't care.
He didn't try to please
        yet got around to doing his share.
He wasn't proud enough
        to be discontented
but took what came with pleasure,
and soon forgot what wasn't there.

JORDAN JONES

Zen Baker

He who bakes bread
shall know grain
by touch & blood

of fiber shall expand
his heart as he leans
to knead. Dough,

secret & liquid,
shall flow toward the hot stoves
of his hands, teaching him

to breathe, to push & pull
a loaf into shape
from within,

as he dances without.
He shall hide
behind his apron

a belly of knowledge,
rounded alike by deep brown
successes & burnt failures.

GILLIAN COOTE

Tenzo's Song

I'm just a big old rusty wok
scrape me away till I'm clean

a handful of chinese vegetables
sizzle me in sesame oil

two fighting goannas
scratch my eyes out, bite my neck

the bell that starts zazen
rings and rings through space and time

that cut!   that Kaaatz!
that slices through

the magpie chant
that fills the valley.

AL ROBLES

Ryokan the Crazy Snow Poet

Reading this poet makes me wonder who's crazy?
They say he was born in 1758 in the village of
Izumozaki in Echigo province now called Niigata
on the northwest coast of Japan. They called him

Eizo when he was a child. There are times when
I feel like Ryokan running free and crazy in the snow.
I didn't know until later how crazy I was
Stripping down naked ... running wild through big
bear snow country. I dug a hole and laid down
my mind. Remembering how Ryokan lived in his shack ...
He drank tea around the clock. A few years back
I carried rocks from the Tuoloumne River and
gathered wood all year round for a tea house. That's
crazy! Ryokan was a simple poet who believed in
mountain snow-silence and the freedom to be himself.
Nothing else really matters.

NINA WISE

To Papaji*

I looked for you all my life
by 747, bullet train, camel back, by foot;
snatched fractured glimpses
that burrowed beneath my skin.

I looked for you everywhere,
in bhavans, mountains, monasteries, stones,
fretted koans, ate sweet rice,
drank yak tea, and bowed.

I looked for you all my life,
then found you in the chant
of the tangerine man pushing
his wooden cart of thick-skinned sweets
down dung-smoked roads.

I looked for you everywhere,
then found you in the eyes
of the peanut boy, perched cross-legged
in his once-white kurta, stirring
warm-weather snacks in a roasting pan.

* H. W. L. Poonja (1910–1997) was known as Papaji to his devotees.

I looked for you all my life,
then found you in the upturned palm
of a white-maned man, propped in a deluge
of car horns and fumes, his plastic legs
upright beside him.

I looked for you everywhere,
then found you in the rough tongue
of a wattled white cow, royalty
in the road, sliding a banana peel
quick from my offering hand.

I looked for you all my life,
then found you in the high whine
of a mosquito breaking into my netted sleep,
close as a lover, whispering:
Sweet nothing, sweet nothing.

You asked me, Who are you,
the one who is looking; who looks?
and I traced my name in a field of dots
as it disappeared into always.

So this is love, my memory sang.
The lane so narrow two cannot exist,
you said. Chasms opened.
Hearts leapt

into the molten place where light embraces
form and what matters waits patient
as a mountain expecting a slow train,
its cars dismembered in an accident.

Reassembled, I made my way
to the peak to view the lay
of the land: beginnings, endings,
seasons, weather moving.

Back home, slippers, dog at my feet,
an open window, I find you in the breeze
that caresses my face with a whisper:
Sweet nothing, sweet nothing.

Surrender

at our house there live
a girl, a dog, and a yardful of newly planted
flowers
The dog came free, the girl is priceless
and the flowers cost three hundred dollars,
a cozy scene but complicated
in that
I love the girl, the girl loves the dog
and the dog
loves to dig my flowers
and I

do   not   love   the   dog

creating a dilemma in which I
who crave
even the illusion of control
am stymied between my needs
for the orderly completion of my desires
and
the beam of joyous fire
in the eyes of the girl,
all of which
says more about the complexities of love
than the training of neurotic dogs
and I've just discovered
in writing these lines
that
the dharma of this dilemma
has less to do with my training the dog
to not dig my flowers
than the dog training me
to love
the girl

TOM GREENING

My Children Visit the Zendo

In a decrepit part of town
A rear-ended Pinto
Slumps at the curb.
The Zendo is in an old house.
And in the front yard of raked dirt
Goldfish get used to their pond.
Holding my view of Zen,
I enter.
The Roshi does not console.
He does, however, smile
When asked about fear.
Always the spiritual tourist,
I notice irrelevancies (sandal styles),
But become peaceful.
The next day I return
With my children, who
Become entranced with a cat.
They sit more comfortably than I
On the mat, and
Enjoy the gongs.
I want them to take it all seriously.
When they say, "Let's go,"
I let go.

SARAH ARSONE

A Father's Poem

In my room
at last
I'm finally free
to sleep my sleep
and dream my own dreams
beside your mom
who grows bigger
each night
with the new child

getting ready
to come
into our
lives.

And I fear
with two babes
in the house
I'll have no
time at all
for me.

How will I
sleep the sleep
I need to be alert
in my office every morning
or be free to walk the
solitary paths
I love?

Or find the time
to think my thoughts
with two like you
crying in the night
asking for
water
bears
and who knows
what else?

What
will I do then?

What will
I do?

Just breathe
in and out
and watch
my breath
go out and in
they say.

The teacher
Thich Nhat Hanh

tells
the tale
of another father
chasing down time
enough to satisfy
a rowdy son
newborn-daughter
wife
and self.

That father
meditates on breath
and finds some way to make
the time his children take
his own time too.

He gently twists
and bends the hard
dividing line
between "my afternoon"
"your morning"
between "work time,"
"play time" between "your time"
or "my time"
for all the things to do.

He relaxes
the boundaries
between "me"
and "you."

That father
stakes a claim
to the days and hours
he spends on baby baths
and bottles
games and tears and grins
even midnight
diaper changes –
as his time too.

So he finds
he now has
endless time.

Will I be able
to do that as well?

Only time
and breath
will tell.

MIRIAM SAGAN

"Winter burn"

Acorns scatter the ground;
Hexagonal flower flats honeycomb the earth;
Frost on the garden, laundry on the line;
Lanterns light the pathway in blue of dusk or dawn
A few stars arriving or disappearing;
It is beautiful to see a man and a woman
Sitting opposite each other and sewing by the same lamp

Tassajara Zen Mountain Center
December 29, 1982

DIANA LEVY

Honey
for Anne Aitken

It was a honey time there in the valley
with the women, spiked with frost and stars –
my whole body felt like a smile
as I supped it like a winter bee
and was nourished and healed –
we were all Queens, fattening our hearts –

Afterwards, still on that fertile edge
between one soul-system and another,
I had to do the shopping. I gathered up
my bags, but at the supermarket I dropped
the coastal gum honey in its glass jar
on the hard floor and it shatters –
the current of shoppers sweep around my crisis

in 4 o'clock haste, as I view the bag of groceries
stuck with honey and razor-sharp glass
oozing into the aisles –
the floor has no use for such sweetness –

The trolleys, neat jars of Vegemite,
stacks of SPECIAL!s – I wish
it would all burst into laughter
at this splendid small tragedy –

Feeling boxed back in
I drove home and there learn
that you have died:
your honey all spilled in heart attack.

I'm cleaning up with tears now
as I remember you in an old blue muu-muu,
shopping bag in hand as you
step from the threshold into the street,
your white hair coiled in a low braided bun
maybe a lei of plumeria around your neck
your wise clear eyes and
always that nectar smile
which greeted every being
and every smashed jar.

DAN CLURMAN

The Berkeley Marina at Dusk

Not long ago I sat here with my mother.
Just looking at the waters was
enough, she said.

Now, I feel the breath of life
rise and fall with the ripples of the bay,
see the Golden Gate slip into darkness
as the gulls cry.

Men ready their boats for rest.
Clouds drift, thin wisps tufted with pale yellow.
Moon slivers out.

Night settles our lives.

I breathe in my
mother's words, breathe
in the breath she gave me,
give it back now to the bay.

To David

We never did finish our conversation
about God. But I don't think
anything was missing.
I remember reading Walt Whitman
to you in the hospital. You,
stoned out on medication. Your wife said
she had never seen one man read poetry
to another before.
You told me you loved me.
I didn't think you'd die.
We didn't finish our conversation about God,
the one we're having
right now.

SUSAN GRIFFIN

Born into a World Knowing

This will happen
Oh god we say just give
me a few more
breaths
and don't let it be
terrible
let it be soft
perhaps in someone's
arms, perhaps tasting
chocolate
perhaps
laughing or asking
Is it over already?

or saying *not yet. Not
yet* the sky
has at this moment turned
another shade of blue,
and see there a child
still plays
in the fresh snow.

YUSEF KOMUNYAKAA

We Never Know

He danced with tall grass
for a moment, like he was swaying
with a woman. Our gun barrels
glowed white-hot.
When I got to him,
a blue halo
of flies had already claimed him.
I pulled the crumbled photograph
from his fingers.
There is no other way
to say this: I fell in love.
The morning cleared again,
except for a distant mortar
and somewhere choppers taking off.
I slid the wallet into his pocket
and turned him over, so he wouldn't be
kissing the ground.

2527th Birthday of the Buddha

When the motorcade rolled to a halt, Quang Duc
climbed out & sat down in the street.
He crossed his legs,
& the other monks & nuns grew around him like petals.
He challenged the morning sun,
debating with the air
he leafed through – visions brought down to earth.
Could his eyes burn the devil out of men?

A breath of peppermint oil
soothed someone's cry. Beyond terror made flesh –
he burned like a bundle of black joss sticks.
A high wind that started in California
fanned flames, turned each blue page,
leaving only his heart intact.
Waves of saffron robes bowed to the gasoline can.

bell hooks

as they bury the dead
for the vietnamese people

to dig
the grave
of a people

it is the way
death is
knowing no names

this hole in the earth
where we come together
as one

it rains
and so the tears of the women
cease their falling

no longer
do we dream
of a new land

but wait the day
when our bones too
shall cry out

against the striking of the blade
as they lay dead after dead
upon us

THICH NHAT HANH

Please Call Me by My True Names

Don't say that I will depart tomorrow –
even today I am still arriving.

Look deeply: every second I am arriving
to be a bud on a Spring branch,
to be a tiny bird, with still-fragile wings,
learning to sing in my new nest,
to be a caterpillar in the heart of a flower,
to be a jewel hiding itself in a stone.

I still arrive, in order to laugh and to cry,
to fear and to hope.
The rhythm of my heart is the birth and death
of all that is alive.

I am a mayfly metamorphosing
on the surface of the river.
And I am the bird
that swoops down to swallow the mayfly.

I am a frog swimming happily
in the clear water of a pond.
And I am the grass-snake
that silently feeds itself on the frog.

I am the child in Uganda, all skin and bones,
my legs as thin as bamboo sticks.
And I am the arms merchant,
selling deadly weapons to Uganda.

I am the twelve-year-old girl,
refugee on a small boat,
who throws herself into the ocean
after being raped by a sea pirate.
And I am the pirate,
my heart not yet capable
of seeing and loving.

I am a member of the politburo,
with plenty of power in my hands.
And I am the man who has to pay

his "debt of blood" to my people
dying slowly in a forced-labor camp.

My joy is like Spring, so warm
it makes flowers bloom all over the Earth.
My pain is like a river of tears,
so vast it fills the four oceans.

Please call me by my true names
so I can hear all my cries and laughter at once
so I can see that my joy and pain are one.

Please call me by my true names,
so I can wake up
and the door of my heart
could be left open,
the door of compassion.

1978

TED SEXAUER

The Well

I think of you
papa-san, grandfather, Ông,
standing at your open well

there you are, smiling host
to a squad of well-armed foreigners, pulling up
red Folger's coffee cans of cool sweet water
dousing bowed teen-aged heads
eight young men this time, huge, all hairy
like dogs, bearing strange black rifles
(they will not go away) wearing only
boots and floppy war-green undershorts
careless youth from a rich world, blind
to soap water spilling back down the well
your task of diplomacy to keep the soap out
without getting shot

for once
I could see clearly what you thought

as I watched you grin and nod non-stop
like an imbecile, disappearing in that grin
into a sea of caricature papa-sans
I saw something I knew in your eyes
I saw you calling on the god
of get me out of this
I saw in you myself
desperate
to preserve the healthful water

by the trail to My An Binh Dinh Province
1970

The Ambivalent Nature of Healing
Report from Sonoma, April 1995

At the bank a week after the shooting
it's business as usual; you couldn't tell
any but daily life has ever gone on here.
That night I heard about it: felt only
shutting down, a muffled distant metal chung!,
and nothing, not free to be impressed by death
nor life, nothing; but in the next days, found
I couldn't walk near: a force of sadness larger
than two men I didn't know bound me like a spell.
In time, my own dead made their ways through to say
at last, "Nothing you need do for us. Keep going."

I went to the woods where I grew up
one last time too many. Last fall this was.
The woods are gone, completely gone. Once
twenty miles out, not changed in thirty years,
suddenly cedars and huckleberries, beaver ponds,
bogs and deer trails, all the riches of my first world,
all gone to housing tracts, middle-class streets,
poles, wires, lawns, people from somewhere else
having no idea what was there; all gone. They
were babies; now they need a place to live.

In the winter I went back to Binh Dinh province,
to my old AO, to the place where the sounds come from
that charge my ears with trouble out of time.
I went to say goodbye to ghosts of men

I'll always love, but can no longer carry.
I found no trace, no ghosts, no floating memories
of the spirit we lived in then; found everything above
and below that ground under vigorous use of the ones
who live there now. The fugitive past I went to meet
is buried and put to rest under twenty-five years
of busy life. It's been that long.

> The lesson keeps coming back,
> the hardest one: the locus of loss
> is my eyes, not the bystanders, not the land.
> Not those lost.

> Can't take nor bring any of it back,
> can only be   in present tense
> must live, must continue living daily.
> It's alright.

Poem for Tết

This is the poem
that will save my life
this the line that will cure me
this word, this, the word 'word' the one
this   breath   the one I am

Nam Moi
Lunar New Year
January 31, 1995

CLAUDE ANSHIN THOMAS

As
the
soldiers
of
viet nam
proceed
through
life
they seem
to be

encased
in
an
aura
of black;
there
seems
no
other
explanation
for
their
neglect.

A
bullet
slams
into
my body,
I feel
no
pain,
I
can not
see,
the
sounds
of war
disappear –
I
must be
dead
for all
is
peaceful,
then suddenly,
the medics,
morphine,
a poncho,

mortars,
flesh
being ripped
from
legs;
I snap
upright
in
my bed
soaked
in perspiration –
should
I
be glad
that
now
it's
only
a dream?

Alone
with only
the
scream
of
junglebirds
and
the
crunching
of undergrowth
beneath my feet
my
heart pounds,
audible
to
the world;
this
emotion
swells

to
a crescendo
of
tears
as
I
look
about me
for
dead bodies
only to realize
that
the war
had ended,
for me,
more than
a
decade
ago;
god
I wish
I
could
come home!!

Anyone can
come or go
whenever
they like
but I must
sit here
to listen for
the faint
whispers
of hope
that are carried
within the
monstrous
agony of wars past –

mine,
my father's,
his father's, my son,
and his son's –
I look everywhere
for the switch
that will turn this
machine off
but I keep
ending up
with bloodied
parts
my soul hacked
and slashed
and my brain
burning
as if infected with
white phosphorus.

The palm of my spirit
pushes outward
my head burns
as I seek
a bed of ferns
where I
could lay myself
down
protected by
the sun,
the guardian
of my peace,
and lullabied
by the wash of wind
whose undertow
pulls me
out of my fear,
I can
close my eyes now
as I am at last
among friends.

JIM COHN

On Non-Violence & Observation
   for Steve Molnar

be a witness,
a presence that may
reduce violence
on both sides.

be respectful of
all persons.
stay calm.
non-aligned.

listen carefully.
don't argue.
be visible in tense situations.
invisible to the press.

if violence breaks out
you've the right to leave.
you will be used
by the people.

come & talk if asked.
eat the food if offered.
death may take
them at any time.

out there alone
in the nights & bullets
love is a dozen dead
black roses.

Akwesasne
April 1990

THICH NHAT HANH

The Witness Remains

Flarebombs bloom on the dark sky.
A child claps his hands and laughs.

I hear the sound of guns,
and the laughter dies.

But the witness
remains.

LORENZO THOMAS

MMDCCXIII ½

The cruelty of ages past affects us now
Whoever it was who lived here lived a mean life
Each door has locks designed for keys unknown

Our living room was once somebody's home
Our bedroom, someone's only room
Our kitchen had a hasp upon its door.

Door to a kitchen?

And our lives are hasped and boundaried
Because of ancient locks and madnesses
Of slumlord greed and desperate privacies

Which one is madness? Depends on who you are.
We find we cannot stay, the both of us, in the same room
Dance, like electrons, out of each other's way.

The cruelties of ages past affect us now

THULANI DAVIS

Aria from X

Malcolm appears alone, handcuffed, under a glaring light.
A chair sits stage center. He seems to be talking to interrogators,
maybe in the shadows, maybe not there at all.

Malcolm
I would not tell you
what I know.
You would not

hear my truth.
You want the story
but you don't want to know.
My truth is you've been on me
a very long time,

longer than I can say.
As long as I've been living
you've had your foot on me,
always pressing.

My truth is white men
killed my old man,
drove my mother mad.
My truth is rough,
My truth could kill,
My truth is fury.

They always told me
'You don't have a chance,
'You're a nigger, after all.
'You can jitterbug and prance,
'but you'll never run the ball.'
My truth told me,
quit before you start.
My truth told me,
stayin' alive is all you've got.

I've shined your shoes,
I've sold your dope,
hauled your bootleg,
played with hustler's hope.
But the crime is mine
I will do your time,
so you can sleep.
I won't be out to get you
on the street at night
but I won't forget
any evil that's white.

My truth is a hammer
coming from the back.
It will beat you down
when you least expect.

I would not tell you
what I know
You want the truth,
You want the truth,
but you don't want to know.

[Lights out.]

THICH TUE SY

Stone Walls

Stone walls are adorned with worthless decor.
No sunset could penetrate this cage.

A lonely man stares at a flickering lamp;
All the world's history cannot describe his feelings.

Hermit Thoughts

Don't be surprised that modest hermits
Hide among the highest peaks
Nothing strange either in finding dharma masters
Amid boisterous crowds
But stuck away from the world in a bottomless pit
With nothing and with no one to care
Now *that*
That's thought provoking.

A Cup of Clear Water

The lonely hermit does not yearn for tea
A pure heart, clear water, are sufficient to
Entertain emptiness and beauty

Though there are few people in these windy and dusty
outskirts
I share my dreams with the purple clouds at dusk

These poems were written in Vietnam.
1988

ANONYMOUS TIBETAN NUNS

Looking through the window
Nothing to see but sky.
Clouds floating in the sky,
I wish they were my parents,
We, captured friends, in spirit,
We might be the ones to fetch the jewel.
No matter how hard they beat us
They cannot separate our interlinked arms.
The cloud from the east
Is not a sewn-on patch;
The time will come when the sun
Shall appear from behind the clouds.
I am not sad. If you ask me why not,
I'll say, "Days follow days. And one day
I shall be released."

The fragrance of the lotus
Eclipsed by the sun
Attracts bees to swarm
Due to its natural sweetness.
Amidst the ranges of the Land of Snows
Eclipsed by the sun
The greenery of pastures
And the blueness of lakes
Are due to the waters of the snow.

My country wasn't sold, it was stolen.
But we've written letters telling the truth.
We've written oh so many letters!
Parents of this lifetime
Please don't grieve for us.
Our time of reunion will come.
Our country wasn't sold, it was stolen.
We've shed tears, oh so many tears!
Parents, so dear,

Your kindness comforts us.
Our time of reunion will come.
I send words of comfort to my parents.
Don't grieve. Our time of reunion will come.

These songs were written from prison.

PATRICIA DONEGAN

Check Up

Tibetan lamas say
the worst thing you can do
to break your vow
is to rape your mother at noon
on an altar during her period
when she's a nun, nobly born
& a relative of your guru.

No, I didn't do that
but neither did I look
the homeless woman in the eye
as sure as I gaze at these stars.

GARY ROSENTHAL

Ghetto Dokusan*

    5:30 a.m.
    downtown ghetto Richmond
    winter   still black
                  morning

    I get out of the car, but gas
    station attendant disappears
    behind the bullet-proof
               plexiglass window
    as two black guys approach

---

* *Dokusan* is a private period of question and answer between a Zen monk or student and Zen teacher *(roshi)*, in which the student can answer a Zen riddle (koan) and discuss his or her practice.

high on blow ...
                    the tall one wants a dollar
                    for gas, the fat one
                    a cigarette – both happily given
                         no sense of fear

the tall one goes to his truck
to write down his number
should I hear of a hauling job
(the long-shot, his desperation
to find work *"anywhere, even Sacramento"*
– he's got eleven children
& it's the week before Christmas)

         the fat one is mumbling
         & making strange hand gestures
         but when I look into his gleaming eyes
         there's a presence between us
         & fumbling with his hands again
         he says, *"I can't express myself ..."*

I say, *"you're doing fine"*
he holds both his arms out, wide
saying, *"it's so big "*
"yes," I say, *"it's big and beyond words"*
"you understand," he says, *"most people don't understand"*
"yes"
then he gives me a hug
until the tall one comes back
but his pen is hollow
where once was its cartridge
so he returns to the truck

                    the fat one says,
                    "I'm a fisherman too, I come from the sea"
                    "brother, we all come from the sea"
                    which brings him to hug me again
                    until the tall one returns
                    with wet, blue numbers
                                    smeared
                    on a tatter of paper, barely legible

now the fat one wants to write
his name & number, which he scrawls

studiously

as I think, *"getting later & later for dokusan"*

then realize
it's happening
now

DAIGAN LUECK

You want to climb the steps
some night and see the city
from the roof; it's quite a sight,
he said. And it's a smoking area.
So I did that and he was right,
the lights of downtown were something
to write home about, except I WAS
home if home is wherever
you hang your hat; except I don't
wear a hat, I wear a watchcap
to cover this shaved pate of mine.
The city. Ah, the city. Twenty years
exactly since I lived here; and coming
straight from the mountain
monastery, a long time gone, it's
quite a shock. So I have a smoke and
watch the lights, the tall-building
lights and the lights of moving
traffic and the lights of planes
coming and leaving in patterns
above the glow and glitter of the
spread-out metropolis; and
in my ears the din
of traffic, of sirens, the shouting
down below in the streets where
the whores and pimps and dealers
ply their trades. City Center.
Well, I wanted to come here
and here I am. Okay. I knew
I'd have to come to terms
with it one day, have to test

myself, see if I have really learned
anything at all these years away
sitting on that round black cushion
watching, breathing, being still.
Face the world. Find out if mine
are gift-bestowing hands. Go to
the mat with it. You know, the acid
test. Here in town with all of them.
All of you out there.
In Edge City.

LAWRENCE FERLINGHETTI

Millennium Cities

How fragile the flesh
        how fragile the world around it
                this life on earth evanescent
                        deep in samsara
How transient these
                solid ephemeral buildings
        Concrete bastions
                piled up brick & mortar
      Wooden caravanseris
                built on sand
        Crystal cities alight
                Spectral skyscrapers
                    sheathed in glass
                        vaulted in night
        Houses of cards
                in sleeping suburbias
        Barrios of shacks
                made of mud and chewing gum
Fiberglass cars and transient trains
                (prairie schooners into Pullmans)
                        sheeted in oblivion
    Transient their tracks and stations
                their "salles des pas perdus"
                    ("halls of lost footsteps")
How fragile the bodies pulsing in them

            (Each a temporary shell
                housing a life)
    Ballroom dancers (husband and wife)
            statuesque secretaries
                    blonds in porno videos
                    heavies in heroic operas
        Bodhisattvas bathing in Ganges
How fragile this frieze of mummers
            this dumb show, "Insubstantial pageant!"
                Gone in a breath
Pale idols in the night streets
                dance and bound to death.

Ecolog

I put on a diving mask and went down / A few feet below the surface a few minnows circled me / A little further down a few small trout no more than three inches / I lie motionless just below the surface and search the deepest part of the pool / There at the very bottom between boulders / in the very deepest hole / I suddenly spy him / a huge fat grey speckled trout / perhaps eight pounds / perfectly still against the grey rocks / He would have been invisible from the surface / and invisible without the mask / Then suddenly I saw another fat speckled trout / not quite as big / quite close to the first / almost like his shadow / or her shadow / this one too perfectly motionless / as if not even breathing / though the swift stream poured by above it / Summer of the great drought / and this the only deep pool left / in this part of what had been a small river / now most of the streambed exposed / fifty feet of boulders and small rocks and gravel / the stream itself shrunk to a width of twenty feet / The pool isolated by rapids at each end / no more than two inches of water going over at any one spot / Last season the two fish must have made it up this far / then the stream shrunk still more / and here they were caught / in the shrinking hole / now no more than eight feet deep / where they lay motionless / waiting / trapped / their world shrinking and shrinking / Still they lie at the bottom / very still / conserving what they've got / They are fat from feeding on all the other dammed-up stream life around them / periwinkles / tiny minnows / crawdads and bugs / skeeters and tiny transparent

wigglers that look like floating questionmarks / They are full
and don't bite at anything / don't go for lures worms salmon-
eggs or bread / Fishermen don't have divingmasks and never
see them down there and pass on quickly / as we dive down
again & again / and see the fish in their steady-state of
meditation / a final yoga discipline / which could go on until
there is no water at all left in the stream / Then we might find
them / still in swimming position / fins extended / mouth slightly
open / eyes half closed / Or still later we might find their
skeletons intact / in the same positions / baked in the firey sun
/ like Buddhist monks burned alive in lotus positions / Or still
much later another age might discover / two fossil skeletons /
imprinted on the boulders / at the very bottom of the crypt /
as evidence of some former strange form / of a thing called Life
/ And if we stayed on here with them / waiting & waiting /
that later age / might also not be able to imagine one boy and
his father fishing / by this stream / though our two round skulls
be found / with the fishes / Yet seeing now the beauty of those
fish / down there below the surface / so still and lovely / in their
deep dream / dappled in their last deep pool / We fish no longer
/ turn / and go on / into the deeper pools / of our own lives.

Siskiyou National Forest
August 13, 1977

At Kenneth Rexroth's

Sweet William Blake
                        in a book in Santa Barbara
            echoes
                        in the eucalyptus
                                ■
I roll seven chopsticks together
            and in their clicking hear
the sound of last summer's cicadas
                                ■
I look Westward
                        into the end of day
            The Last Frontier
                                still made of Water

KENNETH REXROTH

Water is always the same –
Obedient to the laws
That move the sun and the other
Stars. In Japan as in
California it falls
Through the steep mountain valleys
Towards the sea. Waterfalls drop
Long musical ribbons from
The high rocks where temples perch.
Ayu in the current poise
And shift between the stones
At the edge of the bubbles.
White dwarf iris heavy with
Perfume hang over the brink.
Cedars and cypresses climb
The hillsides. Something else climbs.
Something moves reciprocally
To the tumbling water.
It ascends the rapids,
The torrents, the waterfalls,
To the last high springs.
It disperses and climbs the rain.
You cannot see it or feel it.
But if you sit by the pool
Below the waterfall, full
Of calling voices all chanting
In a turmoil of peace,
It communicates itself.
It speaks in the molecules
Of your blood, in the pauses
Between your breathing. Water
Flows around and over all
Obstacles, always seeking
The lowest place. Equal and
Opposite, action and reaction,
An invisible light swarms
Upward without effort. But
Nothing can stop it. No one
Can see it. Over and around

Whatever stands in the way,
Blazing infinitesimals –
Up and out – a radiation
Into the empty darkness
Between the stars.

Void Only

I cannot escape from you.
When I think I am alone,
I awake to discover
I am lost in the jungle
Of your love, in its darkness
Jeweled with the eyes of unknown
Beasts. I awake to discover
I am a forest ascetic
In the impenetrable
Void only, the single thought
Of which nothing can be said.

THOMAS MERTON

I am about to make my home
In the bell's summit
Set my mind a thousand feet high
On the ace of songs
In a mood of needles and random lights
To purify
The quick magnetic sodas of the skin

I will call the deep protectors out of the ground
The givers of wine
The writers of peace and waste
And sundown riddles

The threat of winter gleams in gray-haired windows
And witty mirrors
And fear lies over the sea

But birds fly uncorrected across burnt lands
The surest home is pointless:
We learn by the cables of orioles

I am about to build my nest
In the misdirected and unpaid express
As I walk away from this poem

Hiding the ace of freedoms

from Cables to the Ace

CZESLAW MILOSZ

Gift

A day so happy.
Fog lifted early. I worked in the garden.
Hummingbirds were stopping over honeysuckle flowers.
There was no thing on earth I wanted to possess.
I knew no one worth my envying him.
Whatever evil I had suffered, I forgot.
To think that once I was the same man did not embarrass me.
In my body I felt no pain.
When straightening up, I saw the blue sea and sails.

STEPHEN MITCHELL

Bamboo

Sometimes I have spent hours face to face with a single stalk,
watching for its essence, listening, waiting on the sheer edge of
attention, until my arm begins to sway in the light wind, and
my brush is blown across the page, along the branches, out to
the tendrils and leaves, the last spray turns into calligraphy,
moves down the lines of verse, and with one final, half-dry
flourish: signs my name.

Orchid and Rock

I have painted them in the same mild tones of grayish green.

The orchid supports itself on its thin stem, under the arch of a long, grasslike leaf. The rock, moss-speckled, is suspended in air, yet it keeps its composure. Each may represent whatever you wish, though I have painted them from life, which has no symbols.

When speech comes from a quiet heart, it has the strength of the orchid, and the fragrance of rock.

from "Four Watercolors by Tao-Chi"

The Sense of Proportion

There are at least one hundred billion galaxies in the universe. Each galaxy contains at least one hundred billion stars. Each star illuminates an uncounted number of planets, each of which may support inconceivable forms of life.

From most points of view, the green earth is smaller than an electron.

All this is happening within your mind.

ROBERT AITKEN

Gathas*

When the children fight in the car
    I vow with all beings
to show how the car doesn't move
unless all of its parts are engaged.

When I'm drawn to watch crime on TV
    I vow with all beings
to smile at my own little drama
and expose the killer of time.

If action must wait for satori
    I vow with all beings
to forget satori completely.
What a relief! Let's go home!

* A gatha is a vow for daily living in verse form that is similar to a prayer.

When someone speaks of no-self
  I vow with all beings
to be sure there is no contradiction –
the speaker is there after all.

Hearing the crickets at night
  I vow with all beings
to find my place in the harmony
crickets enjoy with the stars.

TASSAJARA ZEN MOUNTAIN CENTER SANGHA

Gathas

On filling a car with gasoline:
From numberless ancient living beings has this energy been distilled.
May it burn for the benefit of numberless present and future beings
And not be wasted.

On parking a car:
Parking this car, carefully, attentively,
I vow to help all beings to their resting place.

On turning on the television:
Turning on the television, I see all these images as my own mind,
May all these imaginary beings become Buddha.

Walking to the Zendo:
On my way to the zendo
I wish that all beings may realize this precious opportunity.

On inviting a bell to sound:
May your sound fill the entire universe, penetrating the darkest and most painful areas of life so that every living being can hear it.
May the hearer and the heard become one, so that all living beings can attain perfect enlightenment.

MITSU SUZUKI

Soft rain
on hagi blossom
    Buddha's voice heard

JANE HIRSHFIELD

Each Step

Nowhere on this earth
is it not a place where lovers
turn lightly in sleep in each other's arms,
the blue pastures of dusk flowing gladly
into the dawn.

Nowhere that is not reached by the scent
of good bread
through an open window,
by the flash of fish in the flashing of summer streams,
or the trees unfolding their praises –
apricots, pears – of the winter-chill nights.

Briefly, briefly, we see it, and forget.
As if the spell were too powerful to hold on the tongue,
as if we preferred the weight to the prize –

Like a horse that carries on his own back
the sack of oats he will need, unsuspecting,
looking always ahead,
over the mountains, to where sweet springs lie.

He remembers this much from his youth,
the taste of things, cold and pure;
while the water-sound sings on and on, unlistened to,
in his ears,
while each step is nothing less than the glistening
river-body reentering home.

The Heart's Counting Knows Only One

In Sung China,
two monks friends for sixty years
watched the geese pass.
Where are they going?,
one tested the other, who couldn't say.

That moment's silence continues.

No one will study their friendship
in the *koan*-books of insight.
No one will remember their names.

I think of them sometimes,
standing, perplexed by sadness,
goose-down sewn into their quilted autumn robes.

Almost swallowed by the vastness of the mountains,
but not yet.

As the barely audible
geese are not yet swallowed;
as even we, my love, will not entirely be lost.

WILLIAM KISTLER

Standing Near the Ghats Along the Ganges

Since this is the circumstance of life
and therefore a standing up and a walking
around the corner in order to see

where you are, if you then are in the wrong
place at the wrong time you will likely
be caught between opposing forces

or left alone altogether, either of which
can begin to feel closed in, restricted,
like a kind of death, though daily

these same seemingly inevitable structures
shift and it is possible to see them
as unweighted, uneven, leaving you free

to step from the shores of the nearby stream.
And are we not standing in the waters
of the many rivers? And who is it, friend,

and sometimes ghostly lover, who is standing?
I see that you also are a flowing over,
just as the burning of the dead body

is here a flame of bright anguish,
brought forward, then cracking, bursting
into ash, gone without hesitation

into the sky of continuous beginning.

Kyoto I – Kinkaku-ji

On the raked sand, besides a no-smoking sign,
four camellia petals had fallen,
showed their redness ineradicably,
like the heart of a demon's tear.

Kyoto II – Ryoanji

The blond guide was lecturing to the Germans
sitting on the steps above the rock garden,
how the rocks represented a tigress
leading her cubs across a broad stream.
No one spoke. Only some few seemed to be
looking at the rocks, resting at intervals
in the raked sand. When his talk ended
they stepped down, began to photograph.

Japanese tourists watched in silence.
Then they descended, opened their camera
lenses, let the presence of light
bring images forward from the field,
leave impressions printed on silver film.
In place of the immediate eye of memory
they now would have a book, a frame.

The Germans, then the Japanese, left in buses.
After a time four high-school-aged girls
appeared out of the light from beyond

the temple door, as if from a universe
born somewhere else. They stood. They put
their hands together, fingers pointed upward
in the sign of prayer. After some further time
they bowed, departed. A temple gong gave up
its long, seemingly endless, open note.
Wood was taken in hand, struck against wood,
shaped itself in one instant. The two sounds
met in a truth beyond union or completing.

Raked sand lay at the base of my sight. Each
of the five rocks seemed to rise like the wood
sound, as if they were of the moment, apart
from will, as if they had found themselves
borne upward from the place of continuing
lived for a time suspended, before turning,
beginning to descend, finishing back in earth.

Now I felt free of the ordered line of my life,
standing as if behind this face of person,
each syllable of speech resting unguarded
in my mouth, a particular I might taste,
roll slowly about, examine, clear through
at the rim of the demands of meaning. Ry o
an ji Tem ple Gar den white ground of con
scious ness be neath five in ci dents of rock.

SAM HAMILL

Wanting one good organic line,
I wrote a thousand sonnets.

Wanting a little peace,
I folded a thousand cranes.

Every discipline a new evasion;
every crane a dodge:

Basho didn't know a thing about water
until he heard the frog.

from "Old Bones"

ROBERT DUNCAN

I have
nothing to go on

but I must
get
across

where there is
nor here nor there

"is"
wavers and goes out

to meet you

March 21, 1974

For the Assignment of the Spirit

the secret of a smile

has passt into the mind-store
    into time and mind-change.

Into the center of what we mind   this in-
    formation   we return to see
in the inward gaze, the   rising into the mouth
    of this secret

reserve   returned   and mind-ful

has passt into the hand-work   the eye has rejoiced in
    this smile   has passt this way
    this working of the wood went,

the hidden fire within   rising thruout into a smiling,
    a sealing in the surface   interworking of the tree's life
    and another
mind-life   so that we see   the wood
    and we see the willing of the image
    brought out   into it,

so that the image perfects itself in our
    seeing and we would not   let it go   from us.   The art!
    the art we address

has passt into the mind-store,   into the realms of our musing,
    into our adoring.   Sealing, the smile
    rests   before us

and the mind would entirely   go over to this state
    this image   of an Eternal Mind

more true to us   now it seems   this Eternal Presence
    than the passages, the changes,   the burning thru and over
        Life is
in us,   our living   in using our stuff up

has passt into the alembic,   the devouring chemistries,
    into the working of air,   into the works
of wet and flood,   the rotting and tearing away,
    into the fire,   the charring, the eroding, the earth
    elements

works now the secret of what the

    smile is,

the presence of the fire's work.

the wearing away in the smile,

    that seal too   there

    the mind acknowledging

taking in   deep

*This poem was written in May 1978 after seeing a photograph of a Buddha
shattered in a fire in the Tassajara Zen Mountain Center zendo.*

ROBERT KELLY

Sermon on Language

This – I mean whatever comes to mind when you read this –
is an organization – from the proto-Greek organ-grindo, "the
music swells, the monkey dances" – dedicated to enshrining
reality deep in the heart of itself. Its code name is Language,
and it was invented a war or two ago – actually during the
Second Gobi War, the one that ended the paleolithic – to confer
on sunlight such blessings as "It is sunning," or "The sun is

raining," or "Shine happens," according to the bylaws of your local lodge. For individual languages – like Basque or Xhosa or Cantonese or French – are in fact created and sustained as lodges of the ancient freemasonic society of Speakers, the ones with Language on their side, the so-called humans. All other societies – and every form of society – is subsidiary to this, this elegant and persuasive artifact which self-embeds its rules and bylaws at once in every member who pays the dues of breath – what we call speaking. You do not have to think very long or hard to learn that all mysteries are ensconced in language and extractable from language, and that obedience to the intricacies of language in turn reveals the exact astro-dynamic efflorescent energy of place and circumstance we nickname Truth. The conjuncture. The lock. The habit the heart wears in the market, the song it hums in the bathroom, the text encoded in its midnight snores. Language is astrology indoors, it is the moon in the bedroom and the sun in your pocket, its rules are your rules and there is hardly a rumor – though there is a rumor – of anyone disobedient to its prescriptions. Timid Nietzsche and meek Blake followed its laws like lambs, and Lenin lay down with De Maistre to graze on public language. Only the one – there was one – who woke up to the sleep of named things ever broke the lodge law and got away with it. All the way away. Fainting, we follow.

Holy Sonnet

Thankmeal our grace is given
Back-pats glib to bless a benefactor
Built before the world, a "lamb"
He said, with intelligent eyes
A devious metaphor, a man who died
Then stopped being dead, a rise
In the rhythm of the mind, come clear.
I wish I could. There is only heart,
Heart and blue women in the street
Whose feet move centimeters above the stone.
Only I mean one heart I mean, a thought
Nestled in the chambers of its care
Different from I am. You want simple?
There is a light that nothing knows.

from *The Flowers of Unceasing Coincidence*

164
Now up in Kalu's Temple
Where the hill is bright in mist,
There's a dark-cloaked Dharmapala
Who'll help my mind untwist,

And halfway to Darjeeling
You can hear my passion die;
(It's true I swore I loved her –
but who did I mean by "I?")

So come and make me silent
Where the butter lamps are hot,
Let me listen to the clouds decide
What is real and what is not.

Since what I see is fugitive
And what I see it with won't stay,
Puff me out and let me live

222
To be in not to be –
That is the answer.

550
o Language you
first Other
leading us
to every other

563
one candle
in a glass
left burning
to illuminate
every being who has ever lived

630
till we make our own land holy
stripped of race and demiurge
this is not abstract singing
in the Dome of the Rock demon faces carved
near the place said to be the tomb of God
a word is something that happens to you

664
in between incarnations
Darwin in the Bardo
dreaming the necessity of Forms
the world is what always comes back

666
on the other hand in other words
in other hands these words are different
things I should certainly have known –
about me a white face a deep
green eye inside a cavern meant to catch
honey-swigging fish and turn them loose,
my Porphyry, in the monk's pond of my fancy
and all the while it was I who was shouting
like spring thunder in stone jars under water

CHARLES STEIN

My hat vanished.

When that cat that
sat up looked straight at it

that hat had had it.

from "Being Mice"

SHINKICHI TAKAHASHI

Words

I don't take your words
Merely as words
Far from it.

I listen
To what makes you talk –
Whatever that is –
And me listen.

GARY WARNER

midnight percussion
ticking grandfather clock
and dripping faucets

JOHN CAGE

10"*
              There is no
20"
    such thing as silence. Something is al-

    ways happening that makes a sound.

    No one can have an idea
30"
    once he starts really listening.

    It is very simple but extra-urgent

    The Lord knows whether or not

    the next

from "45' for a Speaker"

* In musical notation, ' = minutes, " = seconds.

LESLIE SCALAPINO

A man getting on a bus carrying a huge sack of crushed cans
he'd collected for a living barely get the garbage through the
bus door – spilling the cans, the passengers who're the same
as him make minute motion inside of them of beginning to get
down and pick up the cans – decide not to move forward and
he does it.

    Picks up the cans in the bus moving.

    Their not moving.

    Going by gutted area.

    And the bus continuing.

    Man he's only fifty then digs up at night the pipes the men
from the sewage system had worked on to hook up to the
sewage. The person who says this having looked out the window
at the sewage men digging in a trench in the sheets of rain.
And the man coming home there from work at night digging
them up again that night in the rain finds only two pipes are
hooked to it. She says that to them the next day so they come
back and do it.

    How could you know that, they say to her
and she says he dug them up.

YOKO ONO

Painting To Be Constructed In Your Head

Go on transforming a square canvas
in your head until it becomes a
circle. Pick out any shape in the
process and pin up or place on the
canvas an object, a smell, a sound,
or a colour that comes to your mind
in association with the shape.

1962 spring

Painting To Hammer A Nail

Hammer a nail into a mirror, a piece of
glass, a canvas, wood or metal every

morning. Also, pick up a hair that came
off when you combed in the morning and
tie it around the hammered nail. The
painting ends when the surface is
covered with nails.

1961 winter

Smoke Painting

Light canvas or any finished painting
with a cigarette at any time for any
length of time.
See the smoke movement.
The painting ends when the whole
canvas or painting is gone.

1961 summer

TAKEHISA KOSUGI

Micro 1

Wrap a live microphone with a very large
sheet of paper. Make it a tight bundle.
Keep the microphone live for another five minutes.

Chironomy

Put out a hand from a window for a long time. ☞

Manodharma with Mr. Y.

Watch over every part of Mr. Y's body about
10 cm. apart when he brushes his teeth.
If it is dark, a flashlight may be used.
If it is bright, a magnifying glass may be used.

Anima 1

Roll up a long cord.

Organic Music

Breathe by oneself or have something breathed
for the number of times which you have decided
at the performance.
Each number must contain breathe-in-hold-out.
Instruments may be used incidentally.

Theater Music

Keep walking intently.

MIEKO SHIOMI (CHIEKO)

Passing Music for a Tree

Pass by a tree
or let some object pass by a tree
but each time differently.

July 1964

Disappearing Music for Face

smile ——————————> stop smiling

Event for Late Afternoon

Suspend a violin with a long rope
from the roof of a building
till it nearly touches the ground.

Mirror

Stand on the sandy beach with your back to the sea.
Hold a mirror in front of your face and look into it.
Step back to the sea and enter into the water.

Portrait Piece

Do this piece with a portrait of your dearest one.
Crumple up the portrait without tearing it.
Smooth it.
Look at the face in the portrait, crumpling and smoothing it.
Look at the face through a magnifying glass.

Music For Two Players II

In a closed room
pass over 2 hours
in silence

(They may do anything but speak.)

1963

ALLAN KAPROW

Suppose you telephone your own answering
device and leave a message that you called –
you might learn something about yourself.

Suppose you offer to sweep a friend's house,
and then spread the gathered dust through
your own place – you might learn something
about friendship.

Suppose you watch a clear sky and wait for a
cloud to form – you might learn something
about nature. Suppose you wait longer, for
the sky to clear – you might learn something
else about yourself.

LAURIE ANDERSON

Wild White Horses

In the Tibetan map of the world, the world is a circle and at the center there is an enormous mountain guarded by four gates. And when they draw a map of the world, they draw the map in sand, and it takes months and then when the map is finished, they erase it throw the sand into the nearest river.

Last fall the Dalai Lama came to New York City to do a two-week ceremony called the Kalachakra which is a prayer to heal the earth. And woven into these prayers were a series of vows that he asked us to take and before I knew it I had taken a vow to be kind for the rest of my life. And I walked out of there and I thought: "For the rest of my life?? What have I done? This is a disaster!"

And I was really worried. Had I promised too much? Not enough? I was really in a panic. They had come from Tibet for the ceremony and they were walking around midtown in their new brown shoes and I went up to one of the monks and said, "Can you come with me to have a cappuccino right now and talk?" And so we went to this little Italian place. He had never had coffee before so he kept talking faster and faster and I kept saying, "Look, I don't know whether I promised too much or too little. Can you help me please?"

And he was really being practical. He said, "Look, don't limit yourself. Don't be so strict! Open it up!" He said, "The mind is a wild white horse and when you make a corral for it make sure it's not too small. And another thing: When your house burns down, just walk away. And another thing: Keep your eyes open.

And one more thing: Keep moving. Cause it's a long way home.

AMY CHAMP

... Buddha is neither asian nor male. she could be an african woman. memorabilia awaits from pilgrimages to places where the buddha sat. that was before he was incarnated as an african woman. the majority of the iconography is asian but reaching for the truth is shopping for colorblindness. in the age of post-culture, even RELIGION must become non-essentialist. therefore the practice has to be adapted to the environment. you are a tree. how much water depends on type of soil. don't need a hairbrush anymore. making a quilt is also practice like meditation, the slowing down, continuing, handicraft persistence in technoworld. or writing quasi-episodic documentary about foreign places. foreign I think is ten dollars in bank account. personal identification number, uh yes, I think it's in here somewhere.

Landing
My insides wait, when the spring rains come and the dogs bark. I wait for space and dark faces and colors to splash the walls smash the computer. a buddha is a lullaby nest, a carrying thatch, a world, not ASIA, universe, a foreverness, never now, but YES, a realistic approach to the material. it's a gift. a buddha is a sponge. a soft approach. a velvet tip-toe, the underbrush. the buddha is a statue and a buddha is not afraid to wait. A buddha trusts not memory, yet knows the child will someday become an ancestor. One time I was sitting in a hut and was holding the mbira and the old woman blessed me and all the magic and essence made itself known. The woman sang a song. "Go into the forest and stay alone." Stars were shooting out of my arms and became galaxies. My bottom half was round and grounded.

Absolute value
The mathematical notion as applied to a word, in order to undermine the idea of there being such a thing. e.g.: woman, Africa, buddha. It's a dream, and me and the dalai lama are in a garage. he's very young and wearing a leather jacket. he's asking us our most memorable experience of an earlier part of the dream. I said, when the radio got stuck on the Portuguese channel and I don't speak portuguese. it was a warrior's training camp. we went through exercises with the monks and they yelled in the inigo montoya voice from the princess bride "PREPARE TO DIE! PREPARE TO DIE!" Absolute value: the mathematical notion as applied to a word, in order to undermine the idea of there being such a thing. Zanzibar is motorbikes and salama sana ... nothing grows out here in the sand.

■

... the mountains of Nepal never seemed closer than when I socialized with African Buddhists. Most of them are European. Hearts of Gold. The second-, third-, fourth- generation dealing with national karmic debt the size of something bigger than anything I'd ever seen. Apartheid tipped the scale for Africa's karma. How to heal the negativity? One by One. I saw the bodies drop in the temple and saying yes today is never too late. This is how the Buddha moved to Africa. Through Kenya & Lesotho, an Irishman who took me in. We had more wine. He had done a weekend of meditation. We cooked something really good. There was a woman named someone. We sat at a picnic table out back. I looked over the fence of the flats. So this is Maseru, the capital of Lesotho. Slow, slow, slow. Poor, poor, poorer than the townships but the people have their land. They told me about the dam going up to divert the water to South Africa and how a whole village got stranded when they let the river flood. I'm watching the bodies drop into the Ganges as I ride that horse through Malealea Valley. As I learn how to play cricket, as the mountains wait and the waterfalls drop ... I am climbing precipices and counting frequent flyer miles. I am letting the boundaries collapse. I am looking for another patient man. I am learning to be human ...

from Vote For Sun, *a performance piece*

STEVE SANFIELD

Walking in the rain
seeing everything to be done
when it stops

MANZAN

One minute of sitting, one inch of Buddha.
Like lightning, all thoughts come and pass.
Just once look into your mind-depths.
Nothing else has ever been.

ounce code orange
a
    the
        ohm
trilobite trilobites

                    ■

There's no question of meaning, in the sense of explaining and understanding this poem. Hopefully, it's a unique object, not just an object. Language isn't just objects, it moves.

    "Ounce code orange": ways of measuring, in a sense. Weight, a symbol system, a color. "A/the": the indefinite article, the definite article. "Ohm" is the unit of electrical resistance, a quality of metal, let's say, that requires a certain amount of juice to go through. In other words, this is a fuzzy, resistant word. It hangs down here, it affects particularly this space. I wanted these things hanging in the middle because they could adhere to words in either the top line or the bottom line. "*The* ounce," "*a/the* code," "*the* orange." You can't say "a ounce" or "a orange" practically. You can say "a code." So there are those vectors going there. "Trilobites": You know what a trilobite is, it's an early animal of the Paleozoic Age that was a crustacean divided into three lobes. As a word, to me it's completely irreducible. What are you going to do with it? "A trilobite": it's like a clinker. Angular, uneven, heavy word. So I made a plural, and I also say, "trilobite trilobites." That second trilobite becomes a verb. And I feel, as Fenollosa points out, that every noun is a verb, and vice versa, and there really are a hell of a lot of them in the English language which don't connect except in being the same word, like the word "saw." "I saw the saw." What sense does that make? Wonderful to work with, though. I also found out later that "ounce" is the name for a kind of leopard. I think it's Indian, or Tibetan. It's a cat called an ounce. So you think of "ounce." There are these words that begin to adhere and appear like ghost around these things. Ounce, pounce, bounce. "Code" – I don't know, that's beginning to seem a little neutral to me. "Orange": the color *and* the round thing, the fruit. Now that I've said that, the word "ounce" begins to seem round to me. "A trilobite," "*the* trilobites." That's how that goes. And this is the dead spot of the poem, the resistance: "Ohm." And it's almost like the "Om," the balance.

Excerpted from a talk, "Arrangement," *given by the poet July 19, 1977, at the Jack Kerouac School of Disembodied Poetics, The Naropa Institute.*

listene
secting
erences

miliari
ontempt
opposit

compani
bilitie
pontane

nerousl
ercussi
ndition

aluable
rievable
fluence

berness
ionalis
deliber

<pre>
        by   a   I
               of   to
       on   no
    we   or   by
       a   I   of
          to   on
       no   we   or
</pre>

JACKSON MAC LOW

galactic anachronisms enslave assessments

from "125 Postcard Poems"
September 25 – October 3, 1992

Twenties 3

Theater treat it set threat
west of went I let is
polka swollen roar cornucopia tangle
land sought handkerchief reaper

Trim wait flicker rinse
zinc toxic swap
region stretch gamble wagon peal
list wine-red kin

When they cast swan bundle
banter wheel wind
street critical tube leap chafe
reel also vest implode amidst

Vaccine estate merit
canvas leopard approach vent
she question leverage ask
impulse cultivate repute

the poem, the resistance: "Ohm." And it's almost like the "Om," the balance.

Excerpted from a talk, "Arrangement," *given by the poet July 19, 1977, at the Jack Kerouac School of Disembodied Poetics, The Naropa Institute.*

listene
secting
erences

miliari
ontempt
opposit

compani
bilitie
pontane

nerousl
ercussi
ndition

aluable
rievable
fluence

berness
ionalis
deliber

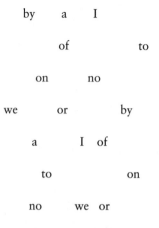

JACKSON MAC LOW

galactic anachronisms enslave assessments

from "125 Postcard Poems"
September 25 – October 3, 1992

Twenties 3

Theater treat it set threat
west of went I let is
polka swollen roar cornucopia tangle
land sought handkerchief reaper

Trim wait flicker rinse
zinc toxic swap
region stretch gamble wagon peal
list wine-red kin

When they cast swan bundle
banter wheel wind
street critical tube leap chafe
reel also vest implode amidst

Vaccine estate merit
canvas leopard approach vent
she question leverage ask
impulse cultivate repute

Visible a rung sank tentative swell
tease wintered antic
vapid assiduous palace accurate
limp illusory wait felt falter

New York
February 24, 1989

awakening

from "125 Postcard Poems"
September 25 – October 3, 1992

PAUL REPS

pine needling

```
                        A
                       ABA
                      ABCBA
                     ABCDCBA
                    ABCDEDCBA
                   ABCDEFEDCBA
                  ABCDEFGFEDCBA
                 ABCDEFGHGFEDCBA
                ABCDEFGHIHGFEDCBA
               ABCDEFGHIJIHGFEDCBA
              ABCDEFGHIJKJIHGFEDCBA
             ABCDEFGHIJKLKJIHGFEDCBA
            ABCDEFGHIJKLMLKJIHGFEDCBA
           ABCDEFGHIJKLMNMLKJIHGFEDCBA
          ABCDEFGHIJKLMNONMLKJIHGFEDCBA
         ABCDEFGHIJKLMNOPONMLKJIHGFEDCBA
        ABCDEFGHIJKLMNOPQPONMLKJIHGFEDCBA
       ABCDEFGHIJKLMNOPQRQPONMLKJIHGFEDCBA
      ABCDEFGHIJKLMNOPQRSRQPONMLKJIHGFEDCBA
     ABCDEFGHIJKLMNOPQRSTSRQPONMLKJIHGFEDCBA
    ABCDEFGHIJKLMNOPQRSTUTSRQPONMLKJIHGFEDCBA
   ABCDEFGHIJKLMNOPQRSTUVUTSRQPONMLKJIHGFEDCBA
  ABCDEFGHIJKLMNOPQRSTUVWVUTSRQPONMLKJIHGFEDCBA
 ABCDEFGHIJKLMNOPQRSTUVWXWVUTSRQPONMLKJIHGFEDCBA
ABCDEFGHIJKLMNOPQRSTUVWXYXWVUTSRQPONMLKJIHGFEDCBA
ABCDEFGHIJKLMNOPQRSTUVWXYZYXWVUTSRQPONMLKJIHGFEDCBA
 BCDEFGHIJKLMNOPQRSTUVWXYZYXWVUTSRQPONMLKJIHGFEDCB
  CDEFGHIJKLMNOPQRSTUVWXYZYXWVUTSRQPONMLKJIHGFEDC
   DEFGHIJKLMNOPQRSTUVWXYZYXWVUTSRQPONMLKJIHGFED
    EFGHIJKLMNOPQRSTUVWXYZYXWVUTSRQPONMLKJIHGFE
     FGHIJKLMNOPQRSTUVWXYZYXWVUTSRQPONMLKJIHGF
      GHIJKLMNOPQRSTUVWXYZYXWVUTSRQPONMLKJIHG
       HIJKLMNOPQRSTUVWXYZYXWVUTSRQPONMLKJIH
        IJKLMNOPQRSTUVWXYZYXWVUTSRQPONMLKJI
         JKLMNOPQRSTUVWXYZYXWVUTSRQPONMLKJ
          KLMNOPQRSTUVWXYZYXWVUTSRQPONMLK
           LMNOPQRSTUVWXYZYXWVUTSRQPONML
            MNOPQRSTUVWXYZYXWVUTSRQPONM
             NOPQRSTUVWXYZYXWVUTSRQPON
              OPQRSTUVWXYZYXWVUTSRQPO
               PQRSTUVWXYZYXWVUTSRQP
                QRSTUVWXYZYXWVUTSRQ
                 RSTUVWXYZYXWVUTSR
                  STUVWXYZYXWVUTS
                   TUVWXYZYXWVUT
                    UVWXYZYXWVU
                     VWXYZYXWV
                      WXYZYXW
                       XYZYX
                        YZY
                         Z
```

Six Characters from the *Heart Sutra*

1. Kan (observe)

2. Ji (self)

3. Zai (being at ease)

4. Gyō (practice)

5. Li (time)

6. Sho (illuminate)

PAUL REPS

well
silently,
overflowing

who
is

THICH NHAT HANH

Reverence is the nature of my Love

NGODUP PALJOR

The Way

PETER BAILEY

DON'T
BE
SADDISH—

BITE
THIS

KAZUAKI TANAHASHI

Does the brush paint, or does the ink? Or does the paper, the hand, the brain, the mind, the vision, or the person? Or does a painting paint?

Can five hundred paintings be created in one stroke?

One-line poem? Why not one-word poem?

open
here

SHUNRYU SUZUKI

Beginner's Mind

"*In the beginner's mind there are many possibilities;*
in the expert's there are few."
– Shunryu Suzuki

Step out onto the Planet.
Draw a circle a hundred feet round.

Inside the circle are
300 things nobody understands, and, maybe.
nobody's ever really seen.

How many can you find?

PETER BAILEY

PRACTICE

lie
stand up
sit down
it's nobody
else's
butt . . .

young lilac rising from the mud

LAWSON FUSAO INADA

A Nice Place

a nice Place

Outside the rest home,
resting in his
wheelchair in the shade,

my father said:
"This is a nice place"

and I couldn't tell
if he meant

the rest home
in general,
the shadey space
with the birds
chirping, fountain
flowing, spring
breezes blowing,

or the world...

Lawson Fusao-Inada

Ness

In a good mood,
I consider adding
ness to everything:
highway-*ness,*
hill-*ness,*
field-*ness,*
sky-*ness,*
river-*ness,*
sun-*ness,*
space-*ness,*
being-*ness,*

In So Doing

The blue jay
Takes flight
In the pine.

In so doing,
It becomes
As large
As your life
And mine.

Clearing

There's nothing
Quite like
Clearing
Your throat
In the forest.

Keep Quiet

It won't
Rain tonight.
The stars
Just can't
Keep quiet.

Just Made It

I look at the tree
As if I had
Just made it.
I count the leaves.

The List

Where is
The list
Of things
To *not*
Worship?

Forest Family

Pine cones

Beneath

Pine trees

Pledge

Repeat after me:

I

Do

You

We

Be.

(Repeat as necessary.)

JONATHAN GREENE

Ruts

I tell the truck
where to go.

The road tells the truck
where to go.

The road almost always
wins.

Hut Poem #1

Trying to
get some peace –
seems the bees
love this place
same as I do.

KO UN

Walking down a mountain

Looking back
    Hey!
Where's the mountain I've just come down?
Where am I?
The autumn breeze tosses and turns lifeless

like a cast-off snake-skin.

Ripples

Look! Do all the ripples move
because one ripple starts to move?
    No.
It's just that all the ripples move at once.

Everything's been askew from the start.

Asking the Way

You blockheads who ask what Buddha is
should start asking about everything else instead.
Ask about everything.
When you're hungry
       ask about food.
Ask the moonlight about the way.
Find a port where lemon trees bloom
       where lemon trees bloom.
Ask about places to drink in the port.

Ask and ask till nothing's left to ask.

Baby

Before you were born
before your dad
before your mom

your burbling
                    was there.

Annihilation

Cut parents away, cut children away!
This and that and this not that
and anything else as well
cut off and dispatch by the sharp blade of night.
Every morning heaven and earth
are heaped up with dead things.
Our job is to bury them all day long

and establish there a new world.

In a temple's main hall

Down with Buddha!
Down with handsome, well-fed Buddha!
What's he doing up there with that oh so casually
       elegant wispy beard?
Next
break down that painted whore of a crossbeam!

A dragon's head? What use is that, a dragon's head?
Tear down that temple,
drive out the monks,
turn it all into dust and maggots!
Phooey!

Buddha with nothing, that's real Buddha!
Our foul-mouthed Seoul street-market mother,
she's real Buddha!
We're all of us Buddhabuddhabuddha real!
Living Buddha? One single cigarette, now
there's a real cool Holy Buddha!

No, not that either.
For even supposing this world were a piece of cake,
with everyone living it up and living well,
all equally able to rig themselves out
        in high-class gear,
with lots and lots of goods produced thanks
        to Korean-American technological collaboration,
each one able to live freely, with no robbing of rights,
Paradise, even,
Paradise, even,
utter Eden unequaled, all plastered with jewels,
still, even then,
day after day people would have to change the world.
Why, of course, in any case,
day after day this world must all be overturned
and renewed to become a newly blooming lotus flower.
And that is Buddha.

Down for sure with those fifteen hundred years
rolling on foolish, rumbling along:

time fast asleep like stagnant water that stinks and stinks.

ATANU DEY

The Buddha and I

I met the Buddha in a dream
I asked him to tell me

Why it seemed so real
Although it was just a dream?
He smiled with compassion
And spread his palms
From which dropped one
Perfect pearl ...

I picked up the pearl
And looked inside
And saw within it
Me standing in front of
The Buddha ...

November 1992

PETER LEVITT

The Measure

To take the measure
of stone give
your hand's full
flesh to it, feel
with your skin,
shape, heft,
and size,
find that part
of you where
it lies, that
field which discovers
you, you there
after all
most ancient
conglomerate
of space,
and that other
thing: what has grown
in the heart,
simply hard.
Do not make it
a crime. Make

nothing other
than it is –
the breath
in your mouth,
full reach
of the world.

from *100 Butterflies*

No life but this one.
Tall grasses
bow in the wind.

On my altar
smoke drifts past the wing
of a clay bird. Mind
is like this, not knowing
where to perch or sing.

The bell
speaks
for itself

Though she is deaf
that girl sees prayers
whisper in the trees

Watermelons and Zen students
grow pretty much the same way.
Long periods of sitting
till they ripen and grow
all juicy inside, but
when you knock them on the head

to see if they're ready –
sounds like nothing's going on.

four hundred hairs of a brush
paint one bamboo leaf
the stroke lasts ten thousand years

My robe hangs in the garden,
dripping like a tree.
One day I'll step
out of my body
exactly like this.

It's easy to die.
Just give your breath
back to the trees
and the wind.

Mother, you were born
so I was born.
You will die
and I will follow you there.
How can I thank you,
all this time
preparing the ground?

within each petal
the sound of rain

Walking the path
of spring moss –
each footstep asks
to be forgiven

Before falling to the scythe
the weeds
enjoy a little breeze

Where you are going
and the place you stay
come to the same thing.
What you long for
and what you've left behind
are as useless as your name.
Just one time, walk out
into the field and look
at that towering oak –
an acorn still beating at its heart.

STEVE SANFIELD

I like my poems short
the shorter the better.
Not that I mind the cold
but I yearn for the sun.

from "A Contribution to the Understanding
of the Relationship Between Buddhism and Poetry"

A Poem for Those of You Who Are Sometimes Troubled by Barking Dogs and Low Flying Jets

Reaching for the silence
he hears
every single sound.

Concern
> – after listening to Allen G. read poems about his trip to
> China and express his concerns about the possibilities of
> reincarnation.

It's not that I'm worried
about ending up
somewhere in Northern China
alone, anonymous
splitting rocks for
twenty freezing years
but rather that
I just might remember
how I got there.

DIANE DI PRIMA

black & white cat
stalks a secret
in the tall spring grass

after months of sitting
& working with the children
the blonde seductress has a sunburnt nose
she lopes over the hills in a tank top & cutoffs

her real beauty begins to shine thru

the pine shadow falls on the tent wall
& I see the shrine
as if for the first time

from Seminary Poems
Rocky Mountain Dharma Center

Three "Dharma Poems"

1.
his vision or not?
gone is the authority
w/ which he opened his fan.

2.
raindrops melt in the pond
& it's hard to say
just what "lineage" is

3.
my faith –
what is it
but the ancient dreams
of wild ones
in the mountains?

I Fail as a Dharma Teacher

I don't imagine I'll manage to express Sunyata
in a way that all my students will know & love
or present the Four Noble Truths so they look delicious
& tempting as Easter candy. My skillful means
is more like a two-by-four banging on the head
of a reluctant diver
I then go in and save –
what pyrotechnics!

Alas this life I can't be kind and persuasive

slip the Twelve-part Chain off hundreds of shackled
     housewives
present the Eight-fold Path like the ultimate roadmap
at all the gas stations in Samsara

But, oh, my lamas, I want to
how I want to!
Just to see your old eyes shine in this Kaliyuga
stars going out around us like birthday candles
your Empty Clear Luminous and Unobstructed
Rainbow Bodies
swimming in and through us like transparent fish.

Buddhist Ruminations

When things are bad, there's nothing to do but Practice

When nothing's shaking, avoid stagnation with Practice

When things are good, what could be better than Practice?

Adapted from the sayings of the 84,000,000 Enlightened
     Beings of this World Age.

CHÖGYAM TRUNGPA

Haiku

The beginner in meditation
Resembles a hunting dog
Having a bad dream.

His parents are having tea
With his new girlfriend –
Like a general inspecting the troops.

Skiing in a red and blue outfit,
Drinking cold beer with a lovely smile –
I wonder if I'm one of them?

Coming home from work,
Still he hears the phone
Ringing in the office.

Gentle day's flower –
The hummingbird competes
With the stillness of the air.

November 1972

SAKYONG MIPHAM

Snow Fell Twice, the Sun Always Shone

Incorrigible state of bewilderment,
You make retreat life possible.
Desolate green grass, rolling far beyond
Spring can see the clarity of dew-dropping morning cherries.
Achiness that comes from the fourth session
Leaves one humbled and inspired.
Opening the front door,
A gust of wind, round and billowing
Cold at the edges, warm and forceful at the center
Comes gushing in –
Happiness pervades my entire body.
My joints feel achy –
Slouch and sit straight up.
The shrine is messy, haphazard;
Ordered and neat beyond my understanding;
Simplified to a level of doubt.
To light the first candle,
I smell the sulfur of apprehension
The delight of the spark and flame.
My end of the world becomes illuminated – so simple, so
    mine, so obvious.
Basking in a moment of loneliness,
I watch the bright light of sun slide and mesmerize.
Early morning view:
A spider has crawled into the sink.
Plastic flaps, cold air seeps in –
Karma is caused by a moment of agitation.

In the distance I hear
The labored activity of a small bird making its home in a
    tree.
Ever-green grass is swayed by gentle breezes
And common song is sung.
Meditating on a rock has made me soft;
Smelling wildflowers has hardened my understanding.
Delight in a small crease where rice has fallen
Delight in a space –
Time has become smooth and sweet.
Rise, drink bitter tea
Light a piece of broken incense –
Life is full of retreat.

St. Margaret's Bay, Nova Scotia
1992

ALLEN GINSBERG

Sitting crosslegged on a wooden floor
    above the tiny desk, pine branches hang in rain
before my eyes thru glass – a drop falls from roof edge

broken earth here, pebbles brought from afar scattered
    by white treestump, green grass Crowds the path –

Grey streaks my beard, I began sitting quiet
    lately, but it's too late to read Lankavatara,
Surangama, Diamond and ten thousand sutras –
    Bald head holds no Chinese, Sanskrit, Japanese,
    Tibetan – only Half lotus below my waste,
and now Rheumatism twinges my knees when I walk –
Well, with such pines hung in grey sky
    I still must be Buddha here – If not
        who am I?

May 3, 1971

❖

The moon in the dewdrop is the real moon
The moon in the sky's an illusion
Which Madhyamika* school does that represent?

Rocky Mountain Dharma Center
August 1991

Selected American Sentences & Haiku

The gray-haired man
in business suit and
black turtleneck
thinks he's still young

Stood on the porch in
underwear shorts watching
auto lights in warm rain

Four skinheads stand
in the streetlight rain
chatting under an umbrella

At 4:00 a.m. the two
middleaged men
sleeping together hold hands

Walking into King Sooper after Two-Week Retreat

A thin red faced pimpled boy
        stands alone minutes
looking down into the ice cream bin.

September 16, 1995

Not a word! Not a word!
Flies do all my talking for me –
and the wind says something else.

* Madhyamika states that neither the mind nor the world is either real or unreal.

Against red bark trunk
        a fly's shadow
lights on the shadow of a pine bough.

White sun up behind pines,
        a moth flutters past
                the brown wood pile.

Manhattan May Day Midnight

I walked out on the lamp shadowed concrete at midnight
    May Day passing a dark'd barfront,
police found corpses under the floor last year, call-girls &
    Cadillacs lurked there on First Avenue
around the block from my apartment, I'd come downstairs
    for tonight's newspapers –
refrigerator repair shop's window grate padlocked,
    fluorescent blue
light on a pile of newspapers, pages shifting in the chill
    Spring wind
'round battered cans & plastic refuse bags leaned together
    at the pavement edge –
Wind wind and old news sailed thru the air, old *Times*
    whirled above the garbage.
At the Corner of 11th under dim Street-light in a hole in
    the ground
a man wrapped in work-Cloth and wool Cap pulled down
    his bullet skull
stood & bent with a rod & flashlight turning round in his
    pit halfway sunk in earth
Peering down at his feet, up to his chest in the asphalt by a
    granite Curb
where his work mate poked a flexible tube in a tiny hole, a
    youth in gloves
who answered my question "Smell of gas – Someone
    must've reported in" –
Yes the body stink of City bowels, rotting tubes six feet
    under
Could explode any minute sparked by Con Ed's breathing
    Puttering truck

I noticed parked, as I passed by hurriedly Thinking Ancient
     Rome, Ur
Were they like this, the same shadowy surveyors & passers-by
scribing records of decaying pipes & Garbage piles on Marble,
     Cuneiform,
ordinary midnight citizen out on the street looking for Empire
     News,
rumor, gossip, workmen police in uniform, walking silent
     sunk in thought
under windows of sleepers coupled with Monster squids &
     Other-Planet eyeballs in their sheets
in the same night six thousand years old where Cities rise &
     fall & turn to dream?

May 1, 1978, 6 a.m.

New Stanzas for Amazing Grace

I dreamed I dwelled in a homeless place
Where I was lost alone
Folk looked right through me into space
And passed with eyes of stone

O homeless hand on many a street
Accept this change from me
A friendly smile or word is sweet
As fearless charity

Woe workingman who hears the cry
And cannot spare a dime
Nor look into a homeless eye
Afraid to give the time

So rich or poor no gold to talk
A smile on your face
The homeless ones where you may walk
Receive amazing grace

I dreamed I dwelled in a homeless place
Where I was lost alone
Folk looked right through me into space
And passed with eyes of stone

April 2, 1994

TAIGEN DAN LEIGHTON

Giving Buddha to all beings is giving to oneself.
Speaking kindly feels good and helps improve the health.
Doing deeds that benefit make everyone to see
That in cooperation there's no gap twixt you and me.

In response to "The Bodhisattvas' Four Methods
of Guidance" (Bodaisatta Shisho Ho)
from Songs for the True Dharma Eye,
in response to Dogen's Shobogenzo

All of Us So Close to Buddha

The whole body of the One Thus Come
Falls in the raindrops and drips from the eaves.
Hearing this sutra in the cool morning calm,
Relics run like rivulets amid the mud and leaves.

After "The Whole Body of the Tathagata" (Nyorai Zenshin)

MARIANE BAGGERS ERIKSEN

I dropped something. I picked it up
and praised it that it made me stop.

When I get busy I stop a while
enjoy my breath and find my smile

Don't waste your time – find happiness
in being mindful in your breath.

I breathe the air as sweet caress
and help myself to mindfulness.

I drink my tea with tasteful tongue
and breathe the scent which comes along.

With gentle steps I kiss the ground
so mindfully I get around.

The present moment ends your stress
makes vitamins of mindfulness.

Gilleleje, Denmark

HESTER G. STORM

Bop for Laotzu
No. 9

No good hangin' onto a full cup
you gotta leave go when your number comes up

a knife that's had too much honin'
bends too easy – it ain't worth ownin'

A crib full of loot ain't really nowhere –
you can't take it up the golden stair

if you're a big wheel and bust your vest
you'll end with a bringdown like all the rest

when you done made your bread – cut out
and take time to dig what it's all about

lay down your load –
that's the road

ADAM YAUCH

Bodhisattva Vow

As I develop the awakening mind
I praise the Buddhas as they shine
I bow before you as I travel my path
to join your ranks, I make my full-time task
for the sake of all beings I seek
the enlightened mind, that I know I'll reap
respect to Shantideva and all the others
who brought down the Dharma for sisters and brothers
I give thanks for this world as a place to learn
and for this human body that I'm glad to have earned
and my deepest thanks to all sentient beings
for without them there would be no place to learn what I'm
    seeing
there's nothing here that's not been said before
but I put it down now so that I'll be sure
to solidify my own views

and I'll be glad if it helps anyone else out too
if others disrespect me or give me flack
I'll stop and think before I react
knowing that they're going through insecure stages
I'll take the opportunity to exercise patience
I'll see it as a chance to help the other person
nip it in the bud before it can worsen
a chance for me to be strong and sure
as I think on the Buddhas who have come before
as I praise and respect the good they've done
knowing only love can conquer hate in every situation
we need other people in order to create
the circumstances for the learning that we're here to
    generate
situations that bring up our deepest fears
so we can work to release them until they're cleared
Therefore, it only makes sense
to thank our enemies despite their intent

The bodhisattva path is one of power and strength
a strength from within to go the length
seeing others are as important as myself
I strive for a happiness of mental wealth
with the interconnectedness that we share as one
every action that we take affects everyone
so in deciding for what a situation calls
there is a path for the good for all
I try to make my every action for that highest good
with the altruistic wish to achieve buddhahood
so I pledge here before everyone who's listening
to try to make my every action for the good of all beings
for the rest of my lifetimes and even beyond
I vow to do my best to do no harm
and in times of doubt I can think on the Dharma
and the enlightened ones who've graduated samsara

The Update

I can hear the trumpets blowing screaming out the end of
    time
look around and listen and you'll see every sign

the waters are polluted as the forests are cut down
bombing and drilling deep below the ground
check the prophecies from around the world
and look around now as it all unfurls
look into yourself and see what goes on
get a feeling in your heart of the right from wrong
because the mother earth needs to be respected
been far too long that she's been neglected
race against race, such a foolish waste
it's like cutting off your nose to spite your face
and at the end of the wars, what was the cost
it's clear that the earth was the one who lost
we are one with her as she is one with us
it's unreal how she is treated so unjust
as our planet grows smaller each and every day
everyone affecting everyone in every way
we're all citizens of the world community
all here together and we're searching for unity
over the years, I've grown and changed so much
things I know now years ago, I couldn't touch
there are things I've done that I wouldn't do again
but I'm glad that I did 'cause I've learned from them
I just try to stay present right here, right now
no worries, no fears and without any doubts
it's about time

'cause in these times, these changing times
a transition is occurring and I am not blind
as the pendulum swings a new age we enter
and with every swing, it draws closer to the center
yes the storm before the calm and the wars that lead to love
things must run their course so we push and we shove
but we're here to work it out in one way or another
to find a mutual respect for ourselves and one another
and the true key is a trust in self
for when I trust myself, I fear no one else
I took control of my life just as anyone can
I want everyone to see it's in the palm of your hand
the past is gone, the future yet unborn
but right here and now is where it all goes on
I know we can fix it and it's not too late
I give respect to King and his nonviolent ways

I dream and I hope and I won't forget
someday I'm going to visit on a free Tibet
someday I'm going to see us all joined as one
and it would be too bad to blow it up before we're done
cause we long behind the rage learning from the pain
the love behind the tension like the sun behind the rain
I'm sending love light to all that is
to all creation and the life we live
I'm not preaching bull shit just speaking my mind
'cause I'm here now and it's about time

PETER COYOTE

*Here are the lyrics of an old tune, played around many a commune
campfire. You have to imagine congas, flutes, lots of guitars, red wine
and weed and you'll get the picture:*

Do you think
Think that you have a chance
When the drummer grins
And starts the Devil-dance?
Try your vanities on for size,
While the ants are eating out your eyes.

La-la-*la*   la *la*   la-la-la *la*
La *la*   la la la (repeat)

A rush of blood
A vein turns a corner over bone.
I just got a buzz
from my spinal telephone.
Imagination, it won't leave me alone,
But I never tried to claim it as my own.

If you weep, it's only skin-deep
If you weep, it's only skin-deep.
If you weep, it's only skin-deep,
because:
Every skeleton wears a grin.
Your bones are beggin' you to give on in.
Every skeleton wears a grin.

Your bones are beggin' you to give on in.

La-la-la etc.

(Repeat until everyone is berserk.)

BUTCH HANCOCK

My Mind's Got a Mind of Its Own

my mind's got a mind of its own
takes me out a walkin'
when I'd rather stay at home
takes me out to parties
when I'd rather be alone
my mind's got a mind of its own

I been doin' things
I thought I'd never do
I been gettin' into trouble
without ever meanin' to
I no sooner settle down than
I'm right back up again
I feel just like a leaf out in the wind

I seem to forget
half the things I start
I try to build a house and then
I tear the place apart
I freeze myself in fire
and I burn myself on ice
I can't count to one
without thinkin' twice

I tell myself to do
the things I should
then I get to thinkin'
them things ain't any good
I tell myself the truth but I know
I'm lyin' like a snake
you can't walk on water
at the bottom of the lake

Circumstance

All of what i feel – and for all i know
there is no high – and there is no low
    no standin' wave – no rollin' stone
    no ramblin' man – no great unknown
and there is no time – and there is no place
and there is no form – and there is no face
    just somethin' shinin' – over yonder hill
    and i know not to chase it – but i know i will
        and you'll hear me sing – and you'll see me dance
        a golden ring – around circumstance

All of what i feel – and for all i see
there is no you – and there is no me
    no howlin' wind – no drivin' rain
    no fallin' star – no lonesome train
and there is no fountain – no river wide
no solid mountain – no crimson tide
    just somethin' shinin' – way deep inside
    you can't deny – what you cannot hide
        and i'll hear you sing – and i'll see you dance
        a golden ring – around circumstance

All of what i feel – and for all i am
there is no lion – and there is no lamb
    no spinnin' wheel – no perfect square
    no walkin' cane – no rockin' chair
and there is no how – and there is no when
and there is no now – and there is no then
    and it's nothin' much – this endless sky
    nobody can touch – but you know i'll try
        and you'll hear me sing – and you'll see me dance
        a golden ring – around circumstance

SUSAN GRIFFIN

Summer Night

This is civilization.
We have inherited it.

We love the glitter.
It is growing dark and trees
crowd the sky.
A pink glow comes to us.
There is a yellow line
we must follow.
Music I find my mouth saying,
Music somewhere back there
in the trees.
Something glowing pulls me
and I whisper *heart*.
But we keep on
don't we, we
keep on down the road.

BOB KAUFMAN

... there is a silent beat in between the drums.
That silent beat makes the drumbeat, it makes the drum, it
makes the beat. Without it there is no drum, no beat. It is not
the beat played by who is beating the drum. He is a noisy loud
one, the silent beat is beaten by who is not beating on the drum,
his silent beat drowns out all the noise, it comes before and
after every beat, you hear it in between its sound is

THOMAS MERTON

Be still
Listen to the stones of the wall.
Be silent, they try
To speak your

Name.
Listen
To the living walls.

Who are you?
Who

Are you? Whose
Silence are you?

from In Silence

ARTHUR SZE

The Silence

We walk through a yellow-ocher adobe house:
the windows are smeared with grease,
the doors are missing. Rain leaks
through the ceilings of all the rooms,
and the ribs of saguaro thrown across vigas
are dark, wet, and smell. The view outside
of red-faded and turquoise-faded adobes
could be Chihuahua, but it isn't.
I stop and look through an open doorway,
see wet newspapers rotting in mud
in the small center patio.
I suddenly see red bougainvillea blooming
against a fresh white-washed wall,
smell yellow wisteria through an open
window on a warm summer night;
but, no, a shot of cortisone is no cure
for a detaching retina. I might just
as well see a smashed dog in the street,
or a boojum tree pushing its way up
through asphalt. And as we turn
and arrive where we began, I notice
the construction of the house is
simply room after room forming a square.
We step outside, and the silence is as
water is, taking the shape of the container.

Ice Floe

Nails dropped off a roof onto flagstone;
slow motion shatter of a windowpane;
the hushed sound when a circular saw cutting through
 plywood

stops, and splinters of wood are drifting in air;

lipstick graffiti on a living room wall;

cold stinging your eardrums;

braking suddenly along a curve, and the car spinning,

holding your breath as the side-view mirror is snapped by a
sign pole;

the snap as a purple chalk line marks an angular cut on
black Cellutex;

dirt under your nails,

as you dig up green onions with your bare hands;

fiber plaster setting on a wall;

plugging in an iron and noticing the lights dim in the other
room;

sound of a pencil drawn along the edge of a trisquare;

discovering your blurred vision is caused by having two
contacts in each eye;

thud as the car slams into a snowbank and hits a fence;

smell of a burnt yam;

the bones of your wrist being crushed;

under a geranium leaf, a mass of spiders

moving slowly on tiny threads up and down and across to
different stems.

PATRICIA Y. IKEDA

Wood

Reliquaries the size of samovars holding bits of the true cross,
so crusted over with gold and jewels you'd never notice the
toothpick of holy wood if it weren't smack in the center, takes
you back to faith in miracles, times they'd pray to that fragment
of Calvary, how he got there, from planing wood in the shop,
pushing off the long fragrant curls, the shavings, the sawdust
that got in your hair and stung your nose, the fresh droplets
of sap on the cut tree, sticky as honey and bright as amber,
that's memory, a fly trapped forever like a star in a sapphire,
night sky over the olive grove at Gethsemane, he put his hand
on the trunk, called for his father, I called, stacking wood until
my arms were frozen, loading it in the old horse trailer, my fa-
ther swinging the angry buzz saw, I got a sliver in my palm,

cried, we went home with wood, burned it all winter, the
glowing logs eaten away by flame, an incandescent heart that
looked like miniature cities sacked and smoldering, that's
memory, wood, the stick in your hand you smack the sheep
with and yell at the dogs, we were there, that's memory, the
wood that goes into your house, this paper, his cross, the cedar
chest of a bride who is buried in a box of pine.

Wild Iris
for Chris Nash

I wanted to describe the wild iris
blooming in the hills above Oakland,
how it stars the darkness beneath trees
exhaling coolness in the green spring dusk.
But instead this poem wants to express
your slow step on the damp path
and my year-old son's face
as, strapped to your back, he reached up
to touch leaves, and waved to me.

I know I'm out of touch with the world,
that Eastern Europe is on fire,
the suffering and terror continues,
bad jokes and bad jobs.
I know that some things fall down, others build,
I know how my son fits a cover to a box
as though it were important. It might be so.
I know the wild iris blooms in late April
because you showed me; I cannot guess
what this poem wants to be, growing
long leaves and veiled buds into my life
through chaos and clutter. This poem says
it doesn't want to end; it has strength
like rain, or human loss. It wants
to hold everything, it wants to rise up
amid the ordinary course of our lives.

OK-KOO KANG GROSJEAN

Iris

Even death
cannot touch
such unblemished beauty.

Three petals hold the sky
and three look after the earth,
while a seed of detachment
secretly ripens
in that dark purple chamber.

The irresistible dance
of its petals
draws me into
another world
and I become a flower.

Whenever a thought arises,
the precipitate of desire
remains.

But the joy of a heart
after long meditation
sparkles as dewdrops
on the fragile petals.

Were I a Flower

Were I a flower
I'd like to be anonymous and
wild
hidden amongst pine needles
near a lichen-covered rock
deep in the mountains.

But it would be good
to catch the grateful glance
of a lonely traveler
like Basho.

STEVE SANFIELD

Hills of buttercups
but with one on the table
their meaning is clear

OK-KOO KANG GROSJEAN

Garden

The space
between the leaves
is full of sunlight.

At the sharp edge,
no longer crowded
with past and future,

fruits ripen on the lemon tree
in the silence
rising
from the morning air.

Wind

Like a well-trained soldier
you know precisely
when to advance
and when to retreat.

When you appear as a gale
you are violent
as a shaman entering
the other world.

But in your gentle breath,
the animate and
inanimate
sing in unison.

I'd like to remember you
as a sage

whose presence is felt
but who leaves no trace
behind.

LEW WELCH

Redwood Haiku

Orange, the brilliant slug –
Nibbling at the leaves of
Trillium

Difficulty Along the Way

Seeking Perfect Total Enlightenment
is looking for a flashlight
when all you need the flashlight for
is to find your flashlight

Small Sentence to Drive Yourself Sane

The next time you are doing something absolutely
ordinary, or even better

the next time you are doing something absolutely
necessary, such as pissing, or making love, or shaving, or
washing the dishes or the baby or yourself or the room,
say to yourself:

"So it's all come to this!"

Large Little Circle

Recently I met a friend for the first time in 8 years

For 8 years he told his wife I said certain things which,
all that time, I attributed to him

... some insight or other, more or less accurately phrased ...

"WE'RE ALL THE SAME PERSON!"

Which is something another friend said. It's sometimes
    attributed to me.

1957

I saw myself
a ring of bone
in the clear stream
of all of it

and vowed,
always to be open to it
that all of it
might flow through

and then heard
"ring of bone" where
ring is what a

bell does

Springtime in the Rockies, Lichen

All these years I overlooked them in the
racket of the rest, this
symbiotic splash of plant and fungus feeding
on rock, on sun, a little moisture, air –
tiny acid-factories dissolving
salt from living rocks and
eating them.

Here they are, blooming!
Trail rock, talus and scree, all dusted with it:
rust, ivory, birlliant yellow-green, and
cliffs like murals!
Huge panels streaked and patched, quietly
with shooting-stars and lupine at the base.

Closer, with the glass, a city of cups!
Clumps of mushrooms and where do the
plants begin? Why are they doing this?

In this big sky and all around me peaks &
the melting glaciers, why am I made to
kneel and peer at Tiny?

These are the stamps on the final envelope.

How can the poisons reach them?
In such thin air, how can they care for the
loss of a million breaths?
What, possibly, could make their ground more bare?

Let it all die.

The hushed globe will wait and wait for
what is now so small and slow to
open it again.

As now, indeed, it opens it again, this
scentless velvet,
crumbler-of-the-rocks,

this Lichen!

JAMES LAUGHLIN

What Is Hoped for

Around Amida's lake of bliss
the jeweled birds are sing –

ing that all is impermanent
that the self is illusion

may the unbearable radiance
that follows death be turned

to compassion   may we be ab-
sorbed in the void of nirvana.

1942

DAININ KATAGIRI

Peaceful Life

Being told that it is impossible
One believes, in despair, "Is that so?"
Being told that it is possible,
One believes, in excitement, "That's right."
But, whichever is chosen,
It does not fit one's heart neatly.
Being asked, "What is unfitting?"
I don't know what it is.
But my heart knows somehow.
I feel irresistible desire to know.
What a mystery a "human" is!
As to this mystery:
Clarifying,
Knowing how to live,
Knowing how to talk with people,
Demonstrating and teaching,
This is the Buddha.
From my human eyes,
I feel it's really impossible to become Buddha.
But this "I," regarding what the Buddha does,
Vows to practice,
To aspire,
To be resolute,
And tells myself, "Yes, I will."
Just practice right here now,
And achieve continuity,
Endlessly,
Forever.
This is living in vow.
Herein is one's peaceful life found.

You are nearly as old as the number of years it has been
    since I came to America.

I have taught nothing to you at all.
I have done nothing for you at all.

But,
You have done a lot for me.

I can tell you one thing you have taught me:
    "Peel off your cultural skins,
    One by one,
    One after another,
    Again and again,
    And go on with your story."

How thick are the layers of cultural clothes I have already
    put on?
How would it be possible to tell a story without them?
How would it be possible to peel off the thick wallpaper
        in my old house?
    How would it be possible to ease my pain
    whenever the paper is torn off?

If I were not to agree with your teaching,
Believe it or not,
My life would be drifting in space,
Like an astronaut separate from his ship
        without any connections.

Now I'm aware that I alone am in the vast openness
        of the sea
And cause the sea to be the sea.

Just swim.
Just swim.
Go on with your story.

September 1986

SEUNG SAHN

Good and Bad are eminent teachers.
Good and Bad are powerful demons

Originally there is no feeling, no perceptions,
No impulses, no consciousness.

If you keep It, you cannot attain It;
If you put It down, you cannot attain It.

Do you want to attain It?
Ride the bone of space into the diamond eyes.

Be careful! Be careful! Outside the door
A puppy is whimpering. Don't kill it with kindness.

The mountain sinks into the sea
And from the sea land emerges.
The sea contains all
But depends on Earth.

Earth possesses all
But is without weight
Direction or time,
and depends upon Emptiness.

Emptiness is all, all
is emptiness. Who made Emptiness?
You, I thinking
Discard this. Then what?

The seed is at play with the tree.
The sky is at play with the stars.

TAIZAN MAEZUMI

Untransmittable and moving eastward.
This mind knows no abode
In words or in silence.
The shadowless light of the mirrorlike moon
Is cast beyond all directions
Throughout the three times.

On the occasion of the formal opening
of the Zen Essence temple of the Zen Community of New York.
October 5, 1980

ETSUDO NISHIKAWA

Round, round, more round than the moon;
Keen, keen, more keen than
Himalayan mountain peak!

A congratulatory poem composed on the occasion of
Bernard Tetsugen Glassman being installed as abbot of the
Zen Essence temple of the Zen Community of New York.
June 6, 1982

BERNARD TETSUGEN GLASSMAN

Ascending the Mountain

Standing alone on a solitary peak,
The gateless gate crumbles.
Moving straight up the windy road,
Heaven and earth are walking as one.

Buddhas intimate with buddhas –
What need is there for old medicine bottles?
Then thousand blossoms perfume the vast sky.
Like this, like this!

Protecting the Dharma, purifying beings,
Dragon-heads search for water.
Nothing to protect, no one to purify –
Uphold the true Way.

Eyebrow-to-eyebrow,
Karmic relations everywhere.
Three bows, ten thousand bows –
White plum blossoms fill the air.

The diamond sword flashes;
The shadow beckons.
The only path is descending the mountain.

The gnarled roots are ruthlessly exposed.
Before the heavens were created, this seal is.
After the heavens are destroyed, this seal is.

A formless field of benefaction,
Enveloping the worlds of liberation.

Who has transmitted it?
Who is not embraced by it?

At play in the field of the Buddha,
A solitary eagle circles the big mountain,
Sheer cliffs afford no resting place;
It is time to ascend –
Cloud stepped upon cloud.

Composed on the occasion of his
"Ascending the Mountain."
June 6, 1982

TENSHIN REB ANDERSON

To Bodhidharma

O great mountain Bodhidharma
First Cloud-driver in China
Opening the way of vast emptiness
Nothing holy.
We are still inspired every day
By your gutsy honesty.
You dared to be yourself
And just don't know.

Read by Reb Anderson as part of the Mountain Seat Ceremony
at his installation as abbot of San Francisco Zen Center.
12:I:1986

To My First Teacher

You came like a sweet bird to teach us.
You stayed like a warm mountain to teach us.
You left like fire and wind to teach us.
I came to study with you.
I stayed to study with you.
I will leave to study with you.

Read while dedicating incense for his first teacher,
Shogaku Shunryu Daiosho.

SOJUN MEL WEITSMAN
AND ZEN CENTER SANGHA

Mondo*

Ed Brown: Sojun, What powers will you use to direct others?

    Sojun: One time, in dokusan, I asked Suzuki-roshi, "What is power?" He said, "Don't use it."

      Ed: What will you use to direct others?

    Sojun: You turn me, and I'll turn you.

∎

Blanche: Who can help other people?

  Sojun: Who is other people? It's hard to help other people. Help yourself.

Blanche: How do I do that?

  Sojun: By taking care of other people.

Blanche: What is the self?

  Sojun: If you take care of yourself and other people, it will reveal itself to you.

*From Mountain Seat Ceremony, on the installation of Hakuryu
Sojun Mel Weitsman at Berkeley Zen Center.
19:V:1985*

Mitsuzen Lou Hartman:

One third of my life has been spent in this practice and you were my first teacher. I can still remember your original teaching. One morning I ran into your old house on Dwight Way, waving Daisetz Suzuki's *No Mind* and saying, "I just have to talk with you about this book!" And you said, "I don't have to talk with you about that book. But if you want to go up to the zendo and sit, that's fine with me." Well, I didn't realize it at the time, but that was my first step away from practice "based on intellectual understanding." Now it's twenty-seven years later and not only don't I talk about books anymore, I don't write books anymore, and I don't even read them. So I'll tell you something – your advice was a big mistake. (Laughter) So what do you have to say to me now?

---

* Spontaneous questions and answers.

Sojun (without a pause):
Make the best of a bad mistake.

*From Stepping Down Ceremony for
Sojun Mel Weitsman as Zen Center abbot.
29:I:97*

MICHAEL WENGER

Zen Corners

Case:
Thich Nhat Hanh said, "There are enough Zen centers. We
need more Zen corners."

Commentary:
This comment occurred in Thich Nhat Hanh's retreat center,
Plum Village in France, in 1984, during a discussion of the
institutional and ethical issues arising in Western Dharma
centers. In Asia a place for practice might be called temple
or monastery. In America it is more apt to be called a Zen or
Buddhist center.

Case #89 in Blue Cliff Record:
   Ungan's Hands & Eyes

Ungan asked Dogo, "How does the Bodhisattva Kanzeon
   use all those many hands and eyes?"*
Dogo answered, "It is like someone in the middle of the
   night reaching behind his neck for his pillow."
Gan said, "I understand."
Go said, "How do you understand it?"
Gan said, "The whole body is hand and eye."
Go said, "That is very well expressed, but it is only eight-
   tenths of the answer."
Gan said, "How would you say it, Elder Brother?"
Go said, "Through the body, the hand and the eye."

---

* Bodhisattva Kanzeon can be depicted with a thousand hands, and an eye in
each hand.

Verse:
The exact center is everywhere.
The whole universe is a collection of corners
If you corner the market with centers
You may lose the open field.

JAAN KAPLINSKI

Shunryu Suzuki
a little Japanese living
and teaching in California
couldn't be my teacher
one of my non-teachers
a little lit match from God's matchbox
sea wind soon blew out
somewhere between California and Estonia
somewhere between East and West
between somewhere and nowhere
nobody can find out what remained of him
after the wind has blown and the tide
come and gone – the white sand
as smooth as before – but his smile
from the back cover of *Zen Mind, Beginner's Mind*
has silently infected book after book on my shelves
and perhaps shelves themselves and walls and wallpapers
    too

AMY UYEMATSU

Tea
    for Thich Nhat Hanh

How many years of suffering
revealed in hands like his
small and deliberate as a child's

The way he raises them
from his lap, grasps the teacup

with sure, unhurried ease

Yet full of anticipation
for what he will taste in each sip
he drinks as if it's his first time

Lifts the cup to his mouth,
a man who's been practicing all his life,
each time tasting something new.

Lone Pine

ancient tree
with so many tongues

how long this throated stem
this stillness before rain

ARTHUR SZE

Fauve

Caw Caw, Caw Caw Caw.
To comprehend a crow
you must have a crow's mind.
To be the night rain,
silver, on black leaves,
you must live in the
shine and wet. Some people
drift in their lives:
green-gold plankton,
phosphorescent, in the sea.
Others slash: a knife
at a yellow window shade
tears open the light.
But to live digging deep
is to feel the blood
in you rage as rivers,
is to feel love and hatred
as fibers of rope,

is to catch the scent
of a wolf, and turn wild.

WANG WEI

Deer Park

Mountain of interbeing:

        all alone.

        Hear only

speech-echoes.

        Reversal

            of shade to sun,

              from behind now ahead

on into forest depths.

Ascending these empty hills,
emerald moss

        afterglow.

鹿 柴 王維

空山不見人。
但聞人語響。
返景入深林。
復照青苔上。

WENDY JOHNSON

River Meditation

I am the voice of Redwood Creek
running in the little streams that drain the western slopes of
    Mount Tamalpais,
gathering in the waters that roar through Green Gulch
    Valley,
out to the Winter Sea.

As a river I am small, made of rain and fog
Yet my heart is old, running deep, a heart of many colors.
I have seen the coastal mountain range be born,
I have shaped this valley.
For many centuries I have watered the roots of the giant
    Redwood
trees of these forests:
trees that stood as saplings during the War of the Roses
trees that grew in silence on the Northwest coast of
    California
while Buddhist pilgrims passed from India into China,
trees that reached hundreds of feet into the vault of the
    night sky
while the Dalai Lama was a child in Tibet.

In the Summer I am forgotten,
Lost in the heart of silence ...
Even the mystery of the spawning salmon may be forgotten.
Please remember, though you may not see it,
water is always moving
connecting life to life, calling out your name,
remembering and forgiving all trespassers,
All who do not follow the old songs of the River.

For rivers cannot be polluted;
water is not changed.
Along Redwood Creek there are farm lands;
here, chemicals are spread on the soil, then carried by rain
into my waters.
Pollutants are added to my water
yet water itself cannot be polluted.
This is the voice of the River.

All atoms in all worlds
do not exchange places.

One day last autumn
José Gonzales from Jalisco Province
crossed Redwood Creek.
He was looking for work on a farm along my shores ...

He worked hard all day, planting Irises until dusk
and then was sent along, just as night fell.
In the darkness he walked along my streambed,
following the roll of waters,
until he was no longer afraid.

In the night José saw the lights of Green Gulch,
riding like a ship on the harbor of the valley.
Idilio met him, found him clothes, food and a place to sleep.
All night José heard the river water, flowing in darkness:
At daybreak he was gone.

I ask each of you, for the sake of your Rivers:
work hard to develop compassion and understanding.
Be alert,
Listen to the waters.
We run in the blood and tears, breath and waters of your
    own body –
We can understand one another.

ROBERT SUND

The Frog I Saved from a Snake

The frog I saved from a snake
once, years ago –
Still here, he lives in a little
grotto, in under the Bald Island shore.
When I am out on the porch at night
washing dishes by candle light,
out in the dark I hear him.
Maybe he has wakened from a dream.
The first word comes slowly, but
it comes. Hello there!

Hello, friend. Boy wasn't that
some rain today!

When frog speaks, he knows I am
not a frog; that doesn't bother him,
                    doesn't bother me.
We talk anyway.
The love of rain is enough for us.

Two Poems for the Good Given
    for Jim Smith & Janet Saunders

1
My father –
    He knew
How many beautiful August evenings
surround an ear of corn.

2
And my Mother –
    She knew that
Without love of Earth
there is no love of Heaven

ROBINSON JEFFERS

Carmel Point

The extraordinary patience of things!
This beautiful place defaced with a crop of suburban houses –
How beautiful when we first beheld it,
Unbroken field of poppy and lupin walled with clean cliffs;
No intrusion but two or three horses pasturing,
Or a few milch cows rubbing their flanks on the outcrop
    rockheads –
Now the spoiler has come: does it care?
Not faintly. It has all time. It knows the people are a tide
That swells and in time will ebb, and all
Their works dissolve. Meanwhile the image of the pristine
    beauty

Lives in the very grain of the granite,
Safe as the endless ocean that climbs our cliff. – As for us:
We must uncenter our minds from ourselves;
We must unhumanize our views a little, and become
    confident
As the rock and ocean that we were made from.

1954

JIM COHN

Jemez Mountains Meditation

The brown scrub oak leaf
    splits a boulder like an axe.
Pine needle flattens widest rock.
A snowflake pocks the hardest stone.
The blue juniper berry crumbles
    whole mountains into shards.
An ant's footsteps carve out
    riverbeds without end.
One raindrop sharpens the peak's
    windweary face.
Stardust explodes a canyon wall.
The weight of rainbows holds
    continents in place.

East Fork River Trail, Jemez Canyon
November 25, 1994

ANITA BARROWS

How many million years before wood turns to stone?
How many more million for stone
to be ground to sand? We know more

about their deaths than about their lives,
the great forests that covered the earth
before there was a single word

to name them, generations of silence

of which we can touch
only the last, the fragile bridge

back to what once was everything

from "The River That Mines"

JOHN TARRANT

The Hula Dancers Dance the Hula, Kilauea the Caldera

According to the geological version
the depths of earth
are rock on fire, molten,
that made this caldera
of lava and drifting stream
where the grey cairns stacked by hikers stand
like spirits.

But here, in the vent,
ferns greet the light
with open palms
in the gesture
that makes no difference
between receiving and giving,

and here, in a crevice
stained with sulphur crystals
crunching under my old boots,
ferns heave,
wind rippled, bursting greenly
out the seams;

in fact wherever the earth
is cracked open
among these ropes, skeins
        and giant cow pats of lava,
ferns emerge.

        It's clear
the center of the earth
is made of ferns.

ANTLER

Trees Seen Now

Trees seen now whose roots touch
                tops of trees dead centuries underground,
someday their tops will be where roots of future trees
                will touch.

One Breath

One of your breaths contains
     all the air
         a Mayfly breathes
     in its life.

DAVID TOKUYU REID-MARR

Zen Mountain Center

The early-morning breath
of deer knee-deep in
dew-tipped meadow grasses swaying
in the breeze of
scented ceanothus from the sunny scree.
Turning white alder leaves
on the bank of a seep
cooling the wings
of orange columbine.

Cedar

Ancient cedar
Dear friend
Every year
Watching your balding crown
Above the forest.

Live Oak

Warm tree
Holding families
In its branches.

Condor

Vast sky
of one bird
Circling.

San Jacinto Mountains

KENJI MIYAZAWA

Dawn

Rolling snow turned peach-color
          the moon
     left alone in the fading night
makes a soft cry in the heavens
and once more
drinks up the scattered light

(parasamgate, bodhi, svaha!)

The Politicians

Running around here & there
stirring up trouble and bothering people
a bunch of lushes –
     fern leaves and cloud:
the world was so chilly and dark –

Before long that sort
will up and rot all by themselves
and be washed away by the rain
and afterwards, only green fern.

And when humanity is laid out like coal
somewhere some earnest geologist
will note them in his notebook.

Some Views Concerning the Proposed Site
of a National Park

Well how do you like this lava flow?
not very scenic, is it.
don't know how long ago it was spit out
on a sunny day like this you see the heat waves
just like a huge pan
and the snow up on the peak blue and simmering
say, have a sandwich.
why on earth don't you want to
develop this area?
it's a real good possibility –
mountains all around
crater lakes, hot springs, right there.
Saddle Mountain
well of course Saddle Mountain
and that big crater's probably
older than hell itself.
why sure! you could fix it up like Hell
with a real oriental charm to it, huh
a stockade of red spears
weird-shaped old dead trees put around
and plant flowers here and there.
well, flowers. I mean sort of things like uh
jimsonweed and viper grass
black wolfsbane and such
anyhow, make it gruesome, huh.
tourists will flock from all over.
we could get some mean looking guys
shave their heads
and make gates out of rock here and there
and drag the folks that come, around barefoot
      – you know –
by the "cuckoo singing on the path after death"
and the "ford of the river of the three ways"
"the gate to the new womb" at Yama's office
then, having expiated all their sins
we can sell them certificates for Heaven.
afterwards – at those three wooded hills
we could put on symphonies, huh
first movement: allegro con brio, like springing forth

second movement: sort of "andante"
third movement: like a lament
fourth movement: feeling of death
you know how it goes – at first kind of sorrowful
then bit by bit getting joyous.
at the end, on this side of the hill
hide two field-cannons
shoot them off – live shells – with a bang, by electricity.
just when they're feeling A-1
they'll *really* think they're on the
        River of the Three Ways, huh
us we'll have had lots of practice
we won't be scared at all
I wouldn't be a bit flustered
say, have one of those sandwiches
that hill over there – really drizzling, eh?
like a picture in blue on a porcelain
that fellow will make a good backdrop, huh.

ANTLER

American History in Context

500,000 years ago sleepy chipmunks
    snuggled in their burrows.
400,000 years ago doe
    nibbled ladyslipper.
300,000 years ago
    dust on tiger swallowtail wing.
200,000 years ago
    whirligig beetle whirligigged.
100,000 years ago
    blue heron still as a statue.
50,000 years ago
    male seahorse belly-pouch
        swollen with herd of
    perfectly shaped baby seahorses.
25,000 years ago
    leopard frog on lilypad.
10,000 years ago

male wasp stroking female wasp antennae
    lightly with his mouthparts
as they copulate on the wing
    from flower to flower.
Right now hippo shitting and pissing
    while whirling its tail like a propeller
        scattering the mess in all directions.
10,000 years from now
    opossum scurries across
        overgrown road.
25,000 years from now
    lobsters grappling lobsters
        with giant chelae.
50,000 years from now
    alligator snapper huge mouth agape
        wriggling pink worm-like tongue
    to attract unwary fish.
100,000 years from now
    female praying mantis clasps her mate
        eating his eyes and head
    causing headless corpse to writhe and kick
        till it inserts penis and pumps
    as she continues eating him
        till nothing's left
    but his penis still ejaculating
        in her ovipositor.
200,000 years from now
    yellow pollen-hung anthers
        of a red columbine.
300,000 years from now
    a white pine in spring
        smells just as good.
400,000 years from now
    a black bear sighs
        in her hibernation den.
500,000 years from now sleepy chipmunks
    snuggle in their burrows.

NANAO SAKAKI

North America

At Superstition mountain in the Sonoran desert
A beer-bellied man is shooting
At a fifty foot Saguaro cactus with a rifle.
A couple of minutes later the giant cactus falls to the ground
And kills the man – April 1984.

April 1986.
In a ravine at Big mountain in Hopi and Navajo land
A coyote is reading "The Wall Street Journal."
– How many mice can I steal next year
   From the American economy?

Off the coast of northern California
Sea lions are listening
To the long-term weather forecast on the radio
– They want to freeze-dry the redwood forest
   For the coming ice age.

On a rocky ledge
Somewhere in the century of nuclear power
A family of California condors is watching
"Wild Kingdom" on T.V.
– They ponder how many more years
   Homo sapiens, one of the most endangered species
   can survive?

Let's Eat Stars

Believe me, children!

God made
Sky for airplanes
Coral reefs for tourists
Farms for agrichemicals
Rivers for dams
Forests for golf courses
Mountains for ski resorts
Wild animals for zoos
Trucks and cars for traffic tragedies
Nuclear power plants for ghost dance.

Don't worry, children!
The well never dries up.

Look at the evening glow!
Sunflowers in the garden.
Red dragonflies in the air.

A small child starts singing:

> "Let's eat stars!"
>   "Let's eat stars!"

Mt. Taisetsu, Japan
September 1988

GARY SNYDER

Smokey the Bear Sutra

Once in the Jurassic, about 150 million years ago, the Great Sun Buddha in this corner of the Infinite Void gave a great discourse to all the assembled elements and energies: to the standing beings, the walking beings, the flying beings, and the sitting beings – even the grasses, to the number of thirteen billion, each one born from a seed – assembled there: a Discourse concerning Enlightenment on the planet Earth.

"In some future time, there will be a continent called America. It will have great centers of power such as Pyramid Lake, Walden Pond, Mount Rainier, Big Sur, the Everglades, and so forth, and powerful nerves and channels such as Columbia River, Mississippi River, and Grand Canyon. The human race in that era will get into troubles all over its head and practically wreck everything in spite of its own strong intelligent Buddha-nature.

"The twisting strata of the great mountains and the pulsings of great volcanoes are my love burning deep in the earth. My obstinate compassion is schist and basalt and granite, to be mountains, to bring down the rain. In that future American Era I shall enter a new form, to cure the world of loveless knowledge that seeks with blind hunger, and mindless rage eating food that will not fill it."

And he showed himself in his true form of

SMOKEY THE BEAR.

A handsome smokey-colored brown bear standing on his hind legs, showing that he is aroused and watchful.

Bearing in his right paw the shovel that digs to the truth beneath appearances, cuts the roots of useless attachments, and flings damp sand on the fires of greed and war;

His left paw in the Mudra of Comradely Display – indicating that all creatures have the full right to live to their limits and that deer, rabbits, chipmunks, snakes, dandelions, and lizards all grow in the realm of the Dharma;

Wearing the blue work overalls symbolic of slaves and laborers, the countless people oppressed by a civilization that claims to save but only destroys;

Wearing the broad-brimmed hat of the West, symbolic of the forces that guard the Wilderness, which is the Natural State of the Dharma and the True Path of beings on earth – all true paths lead through mountains –

With a halo of smoke and flame behind, the forest fires of the kali yuga, fires caused by the stupidity of those who think things can be gained and lost whereas in truth all is contained vast and free in the Blue Sky and Green Earth of One Mind;

Round-bellied to show his kind nature and that the great Earth has food enough for everyone who loves her and trusts her;

Trampling underfoot wasteful freeways and needless suburbs; smashing the worms of capitalism and totalitarianism;

Indicating the Task: his followers, becoming free of cars, houses, canned food, universities, and shoes, master the Three Mysteries of their own Body, Speech, and Mind, and fearlessly chop down the rotten trees and prune out the sick limbs of this country America and then burn the leftover trash.

Wrathful but Calm, Austere but Comic, Smokey the Bear will illuminate those who would help him; but for those who would hinder or slander him,

HE WILL PUT THEM OUT.

Thus, his great Mantra:

Namah samanta vajranam chanda maharoshana
Sphataya hum traka ham mam
Namah samanta vajranam chanda maharoshana
Sphataya hum traka ham mam

"I DEDICATE MYSELF TO THE UNIVERSAL DIAMOND:

BE THIS RAGING FURY DESTROYED."

And he will protect those who love woods and rivers, Gods and animals, hoboes and madmen, prisoners and sick people, musicians, playful women, and hopeful children;

And if anyone is threatened by advertising, air pollution, or the police, they should chant SMOKEY THE BEAR'S WAR SPELL:

DROWN THEIR BUTTS

CRUSH THEIR BUTTS

DROWN THEIR BUTTS

CRUSH THEIR BUTTS

CRUSH THEIR BUTTS

And SMOKEY THE BEAR will surely appear to put the enemy out with his vajra shovel.

Now those who recite this Sutra and then try to put it into practice will accumulate merit as countless as the sands of Arizona and Nevada,

Will help save the planet Earth from total oil slick,

Will enter the age of harmony of humans and nature;

Will win the tender love and caresses of men, women, and beasts,

Will always have ripe blackberries to eat and a sunny spot under a pine tree to sit at,

AND IN THE END WILL WIN HIGHEST PERFECT ENLIGHTENMENT.

Thus we have heard.

DENISE LASSAW-PALJOR

Counting Breaths

Aaannghh! Aaannghh!
   Whose breath going out?
My hair rises, I suck in air!
   Aaannghh! sounding from deep
within the alder thicket, dim green light,
   twisted branches
My heart beats faster!
   I grab my ax
and quickly ducking low scramble away
Aaannghh! Aaannghh!
Bear breathes out,
I breathe in
   Gratefully
sharing the air.

For a Moose

Snow twirling night road
within a breath's space
one life, one life gone
covered with moose hair, glass and blood
a moment flashed in darkness, returned to light
impermanence sharper than the blade of seconds
cut between us
would I have known
if Light
            had not returned?
Did you?

Now I understand
in that time
      there is no fear
            no indrawn breath
only clarity
and the result of actions

mind is without borders
skin is no defense against steel

this was the death of flesh
now becoming food
do Moose minds return to willows?

O great Bodhisattva Moose
all sentient beings
thank you
for life.

October 25, 1993

JIM HARRISON

Not here and now but now and here.
If you don't know the difference
is a matter of life and death, get down
naked on bare knees in the snow
and study the ticking of your watch.

from After Ikkyu

DAN GERBER

Afterwords

We say *tree*
for the object that isn't there.

We say *I love you,*
acknowledging the failure
of whatever there was
to speak for itself.

We say *God did it;*
we mistrust everything.

You read these lines.
You think of something profound.
You pay too much for the ticket
and miss the plane.

REBECCA RADNER

I Want to Write like a Postcard

Everything takes a longer time. The rains
here have been edifying. Today the sky
is like bathwater. But bigger. Wish I were.

Like That

I wrote a new poem
Very short The shortest
words you've ever seen
Oh I don't know I guess
I wanted to make it as
much like my life
as I could You know: Dum –
Dum – Dum – But then I
thought that's not really
how it is It's more
like: *Dum*
& everything
spreading out
from that & all the ripples
just as when the big-
deal movie lets out
it looks like the whole
neighborhood is filled
& probably all the city
too & you can take
it from there

KEITH ABBOTT

The Illusion Collector, Age 37

Passion makes the boredom
      of your life bearable (& vice-versa)

Who sees those haircuts I give trees?

The tree "owners" do

My passion for illusion
                    X-ray eyes

Slowly beginning to see the ground
        floor of the skyscraper *life force*

Half an ant
        decorates this page

Front half still crawling
        back half disappeared

Haiku

the grief counselor
        makes a lame joke
in the cancer ward elevator

a windy clear day
outside my mother's funeral
two strangers talk

billygoat watches me work
scratching his wool with a horn
he stinks, too

our honest neighbor's rolled
        a piece of my firewood
back under the fence

what she thought was
a mourning woman a Soto monk
weeding the lawn

drop my new pen
among my other ones
it becomes just another pen

GARY GACH

Inflight
(Solo renga / linked haiku)

Racing each other
one child falls down, so well ...
the other tries it

he sees his friend off, wearing
the identical jacket

outside plane window
glides serenely by while we
sit ... & do nothing

she says she just loves all the
architectural detail

getting up from seat
to go & take a piss ...
... like a tightrope act

the stewardess' smiles
remind me of my wet nurse

they start the film as
they remind us to keep our
seatbelts fastened tight

blink & you'll miss all of it,
crossing the time zone ... so blink
the shadows of clouds
on sea surface ... like maps, on
crinkled blue foil

tasting the new land first by
savoring its fresh water

wake up at midnight ...
don't know where I am, or who!
... return to true self ...

San Francisco – Seoul
June 1997

JERRY KILBRIDE

Haiku

still in the taste
of afternoon tea ...
my grandmother's brogue

the cool surface
of each potato planted –
dark of the moon

firecrackers,
the old soldier's fingers
tighten on his crutch

jumping rope
the little girl and her shadow
touch touch touch touch touch

the wheelchair child
reaches for bubbles
she just blew

the nurse speaks of christmas
red lights on the catscan
go on and off

the harpist
picks a fly
out of her spaghetti

WES "SCOOP" NISKER

No tears and no fears.
I intend to die laughing,
leaving funny bones.

I sit in wonder
at the illusion of self
and the endless stars

Whatever
One word less ...
One, wordless.

BRIGID LOWRY

In the World

in the strange early morning half light we sit
in the cloudiness of our questioning we sit
in our madness and our clarity we sit
in the midst of too much to do we sit
in the warm arms of our shared sorrow we sit
in community and in loneliness we sit
in sweet exhaustion we sit
in the blazing energy of being alive we sit

here with the singing crickets
here with each electric birdsong
here with the rippling of breezes and the dry grasses
here with the cobwebs and the clouds
and the dusty road upon us

us in the sound and the sound in us

us in the world and the world in us

LISA CULLEN

Reasons To Meditate

to practice noticing
to understand simple things
to give myself clarity
to face inevitable difficulties
to make a conscious choice
to welcome my feelings
to know pain
to experience the bliss of effort
to take gentle possession of my mind
to free my mind
to be aware of my sensitivity
to dip below superficiality
to brighten my eyes
to forget how i look
to stop moving
to let myself be how i am
to love deeply
to risk being myself
to sit upright like a pyramid
to stay still
to breathe in the air
to encourage a positive habit
to behave in the manner of one who woke up
to pursue freedom
to touch the ground
to learn without words
to unlock my heart
to go beyond

MARY OLIVER

Going to Walden

It isn't very far as highways lie.
I might be back by nightfall, having seen
The rough pines, and the stones, and the clear water.

Friends argue that I might be wiser for it.
They do not hear that far-off Yankee whisper:
How dull we grow from hurrying here and there!

Many have gone, and think me half a fool
To miss a day away in the cool country.
Maybe. But in a book I read and cherish,
Going to Walden is not so easy a thing
As a green visit. It is the slow and difficult
Trick of living, and finding it where you are.

WENDY LEWIS

It's Like This

It's like this:
               There's this bird
      And you catch it in your hands
      You feel its softness, warmth, its heart
             rapidly beating
      But if you keep holding it it's no
           longer a bird
      So you open your hands
      (Catch it and let it go
                    again and again)

CID CORMAN

Learn to live
with yourself

most
never do

Then learn to live
with one another

even fewer
manage this

Then – if you ever
live long enough –

learn to live
with everything else

NGODUP PALJOR

Robert Frost and I
Have one thing in common
He loves woods
And so do I
But, there seems to be
A big difference
In the way we set forth
In life's journey
He is a goer,
And I am a sitter
He has miles and miles to go
Before he sleeps
While I have years and years to sit
To reach the same destination

Exhausted by jogging
I stopped near a creek
And took a flowing lesson
From the water
And a sitting lesson
From the
Rock

The wish of my Amala
Was for me to become
A Buddhist monk
Dedicating my life to follow
The footsteps of the Lord Buddha

But her wish was disappointed

The wish of my father
Was for me to succeed as
A man of high degree
Earning my life working
For the government of Tibet
Yet ... his wish too, was unfulfilled

Now, neither a monk
Nor a man of high degree
I have no specific wish to pursue
Nor am I giving up to have a wish
Generally, I follow the way of the clouds
I eat when I am hungry
And drink when I am thirsty.

I woke up early
And began my Zazen practice
But, my neighbor's dog
Started barking so loudly
That I could not concentrate
Thinking he must have some reasons
For doing this
I let him bark
And went to bed
Meditating on the sound of
A barking dog

Cars stuck in the snow
Men stuck with cars
Nothing more powerful than snow
Winter in Alaska

M.C. RICHARDS

Snow

White moths in crazy mobs
hunt everywhere
the flame of the winter sun.

EVE MERRIAM

Summer's End

In the still pond
the lily pads
rooted deep
as childhood memories.

Nothing moves.
Only a tiny ant
crawling across a rock.

Nowhere does the world
remain as it is.

JOHN MUELLER

Rubber Eraser

Rubber eraser
in the shape of
the seated Buddha.

He removes errors
in my work.
As he does so,

he disappears.

THICH NHAT HANH

Journey

Here are words written down –
footprints on the sand,
cloud formations.

Tomorrow
I'll be gone.

Existence

It is night.
Rain pelts the roof.
The soul awakens
to a flooded Earth –
a sea of storm
roaring,
then passing.

In that short moment,
shifting lines and shapes,
fleeting,
barely seen.

Before the passing moment tilts
and falls to melancholy,
laughter sounds
in quiet raindrops.

ALLEN GINSBERG

Mind Writing Slogans

> "First Thought is Best in Art, Second in Other Matters."
> – William Blake

I *Background (Situation, Or Primary Perception)*

1. "First Thought, Best Thought"
   – Chögyam Trungpa, Rinpoche
2. "Take a friendly attitude toward your thoughts."
   – Chögyam Trungpa, Rinpoche
3. "The Mind must be loose." – John Adams
4. "One perception must immediately and directly lead to a further perception."
   – Charles Olson, "Projective Verse"
5. "My writing is a picture of the mind moving."
   – Philip Whalen
6. Surprise Mind – Allen Ginsberg
7. "The old pond, a frog jumps in, Kerplunk!" – Basho
8. "Magic is the total delight (appreciation) of chance."
   – Chögyam Trungpa, Rinpoche
9. "Do I contradict myself?
   Very well, then I contradict myself.
   I am large. I contain multitudes."
   – Walt Whitman
10. "... What quality went to form a man of achievement, especially in literature? ... Negative capability, that is, when a man is capable of being in uncertainties, mysteries, doubts, without any irritable reaching after fact & reason." –John Keats
11. "Form is never more than an extension of content."
    – Robert Creeley to Charles Olson
12. "Form follows function." – Frank Lloyd Wright*
13. Ordinary Mind includes eternal perceptions. – A. G.
14. "Nothing is better for being Eternal

* Quoting his mentor, Louis Sullivan. *Ed.*

Nor so white as the white that dies of a day."
        – Louis Zukofsky
15. Notice what you notice. – A. G.
16. Catch yourself thinking. – A. G.
17. Observe what's vivid. – A. G.
18. Vividness is self-selecting. – A. G.
19. "Spots of Time" – William Wordsworth
20. If we don't show anyone we're free to write anything.
        – A. G.
21. "My mind is open to itself." – Gelek Rinpoche
22. "Each on his bed spoke to himself alone, making no
    sound." – Charles Reznikoff

II *Path (Method, Or Recognition)*
23. "No ideas but in things." "... No ideas but in the
    Facts." – William Carlos Williams
24. "Close to the nose." – W. C. Williams
25. "Sight is where the eye hits." – Louis Zukofsky
26. "Clamp the mind down on objects." – W. C. Williams
27. "Direct treatment of the thing ... (or object)."
        – Ezra Pound, 1912
28. "Presentation, not reference." – Ezra Pound
29. "Give me a for instance." – Vernacular
30. "Show not tell." – Vernacular
31. "The natural object is always the adequate symbol."
        – Ezra Pound
32. "Things are symbols of themselves."
        – Chögyam Trungpa, Rinpoche
33. "Labor well the minute particulars, take care of the
    little ones.
    He who would do good for another must do it in
    minute particulars.
    General Good is the plea of the Scoundrel Hypocrite
    and Flatterer
    For Art & Science cannot exist but in minutely
    organized particulars." – William Blake
34. "And being old she put a skin / on everything she
    said."– W. B. Yeats
35. "Don't think of words when you stop but to see the
    picture better." – Jack Kerouac
36. "Details are the Life of Prose." – Jack Kerouac
37. Intense fragments of spoken idiom best. – A. G.

38. "Economy of Words" – Ezra Pound
39. "Tailoring" – Gregory Corso
40. Maximum information, minimum number of syllables.
    – A. G.
41. Syntax condensed, sound is solid. – A. G.
42. Savor vowels, appreciate consonants. – A. G.
43. "Compose in the sequence of musical phrase, not in
    sequence of a metronome." – Ezra Pound
44. "... awareness ... of the tone leading of the vowels."
    – Ezra Pound
45. "... an attempt to approximate classical quantitative
    meters ..." – Ezra Pound
46. "Lower limit speech, upper limit song"
    – Louis Zukofsky
47. "Phanopoeia, Melopoeia, Logopoeia." – Ezra Pound
48. "Sight. Sound & Intellect." – Louis Zukofsky
49. "Only emotion objectified endures." – Louis Zukofsky

III *Fruition (Result, Or Appreciation)*
50. Spiritus = Breathing = Inspiration = Unobstructed
    Breath
51. "Alone with the Alone" – Plotinus
52. Sunyata (Sanskrit) = Ku (Japanese) = Emptiness
53. "What's the sound of one hand clapping?" – Zen Koan
54. "What's the face you had before you were born?"
    – Zen Koan
55. Vipassana (Pali) = Clear Seeing
56. "Stop the world" – Carlos Castañeda
57. "The purpose of art is to stop time." – Bob Dylan
58. "the unspeakable visions of the individual – J. K.
59. "I am going to try speaking some reckless words, and I
    want you to try to listen recklessly."
    – Chuang Tzu (Tr. Burton Watson)
60. "Candor" –Whitman
61. "One touch of nature makes the whole world kin."
    – W. Shakespeare
62. "Contact" – A Magazine, Nathaniel West & W. C.
    Williams, Eds.
63. "God appears & God is Light
    To those poor souls who dwell in Night.
    But does a Human Form Display
    To those who Dwell in Realms of Day." – W. Blake

64. "Subject is known by what she sees." – A. G.
65. Others can measure their visions by what we see. – A. G.
66. Candor ends paranoia. – A. G.
67. "Willingness to be Fool." – Chögyam Trungpa, Rinpoche
68. "Day & Night / you're all right." – Gregory Corso
69. Tyger: "Humility is Beatness." – Chögyam Trungpa, Rinpoche & A. G.
70. Lion: "Surprise Mind" – Chögyam Trungpa, Rinpoche & A. G.
71. Garuda: "Crazy Wisdom Outrageousness" – Chögyam Trungpa, Rinpoche
72. Dragon: "Unborn Inscrutability" – Chögyam Trungpa, Rinpoche
73. "To be men not destroyers" – Ezra Pound
74. Speech synchronizes mind & body – Chögyam Trungpa, Rinpoche
75. "The Emperor unites Heaven & Earth" – Chögyam Trungpa, Rinpoche
76. "Poets are the unacknowledged legislators of the world" – Shelley
77. "Make it new" – Ezra Pound
78. "When the music changes, the walls of the city shake" – Plato
79. "Every third thought shall be my grave" – W. Shakespeare, *The Tempest*
80. "That in black ink my love may still shine bright." – W. Shakespeare, Sonnets
81. "Only emotion endures" – Ezra Pound
82. "Well while I'm here I'll
        do the work –
    and what's the Work?
        To ease the pain of living.
    Everything else, drunken
        dumbshow." – A. G.
83. "... Kindness, sweetest
    of the small notes
    in the world's ache,
    most modest & gentle
    of the elements

entered man before history
and became his daily
connection, let no man
tell you otherwise." – Carl Rakosi

84. "To diminish the mass of human and sentient
sufferings." – Gelek Rinpoche

Naropa Institute, July 1992
New York, March 5, 1993
New York, June 27, 1993

4/5/91

ALLEN GINSBERG

Mind Writing
Exercises in Poetic Candor

1) After 5-minute meditation
   List thoughts chronologically (Recollection of thoughts during meditation): Write down in sequence the main external perceptions and internal ruminations or chains of thought that passed thru your head.
   See: *Mind Writing Slogans:*
   1. "First Thought, Best Thought"
   2. "Take a friendly attitude toward your thoughts."
   15. Notice what you notice.

   Specimens:
   Ashbery "Instruction Manual"
   Snyder "Bubb's Creek Haircut"
   Ginsberg "Mind Breaths"

2) Heaven Earth Man Haiku   *Look At*
   1 Minute Meditation Outside Class: Heaven or Sky
   1 Minute Meditation On Seat: Earth or Ground
   1 Minute Meditation On Seat: Human, In your
                                          Head

   Then write 3-part poem, 3 short verses

   3-Part Short Poem
   Waking from thoughts (Ground) (Sensation) (Heaven)
   See: *Mind Writing Slogans:*
   16. Catch yourself thinking.
   What's the situation (Path) (Recognition) (Earth forms)
   See: *Mind Writing Slogans:*
   60. "Candor":
   What's your reaction, comment (Fruition) (Reaction) (Man)

See: *Mind Writing Slogans:*
    29. "Give me a for instance."
See also *Mind Writing Slogans:*
    12. "Form follows function."
    11. "Form is never more than an extension of content."

3) Extended Heaven Earth & Man, 3-Line Poem
    One Ground – Heaven
    Two Paths – Earth Forms   /
    Three Fruitions – Man

4) 3-Line Poem
    1) What's your neurotic confusion?
    2) What do you really want, desire?
    3) What do you notice right where you are now?

5) Haiku
    Take one vivid moment, one spot of time.
    Express the details in one sentence.
    Reduce it to about 17 syllables.

    Example:
    "Put on my tie in a taxi, short of breath,
    rushing to meditate."

6) Visualization Poem
    3 verses, each one sketching panoramic landscape
    visualized; each verse one breath long.
    4th verse, ending the quatrain – an afterthought,
    zigzag from nowhere, a switcheroo or capping verse.

7) Mind Clearing Exercise: Confusion & Complexity to
    Simplicity in 5 verses of 21 syllables each –
    Beginning with Samsaric neurotic confusion
    Proceeding to simplicity & resolution of the
    anxiety & confusion in last verse.

    Examples:

    Big Eats

    Big deal bargains TV meat stock market news paper
       headlines love life Metropolis
    Float thru air like thought forms float thru the skull,
       check the headlines catch the boyish ass that walks

Before you fall in bed blood sugar high blood
 pressure lower, lower, your lips grow cold.
Sooner or later let go what you loved hated or
 shrugged off, you walk in the park
You look at the sky, sit on a pillow, count up the
 stars in your head, get up and eat.

August 20, 1991

Not Dead Yet

Huffing puffing upstairs downstairs telephone office
 mail checks secretary revolt –
The Soviet legislative Communist bloc inspired
 Gorbachev's wife and Yeltsin
To shut up in terror or stand on a tank in front of
 White House denouncing Putschists –
September breeze sway branches & leaves in a calm
 schoolyard under humid grey sky,
Drink your decaf Ginsberg old communist New
 York Times addict, be glad you're not Trotsky.

September 16, 1991

8) Word Oxymoron Juxtapositions: Re "Surprise Mind"
Take a 2-3 syllable word, write it down the center of
the page 20 times, then conjoin it on either side with
an opposite, an oxymoronic pairing, like "Nazi
Milk," "Hydrogen Jukebox," "Fried Shoes,"
"Animal Shoes," "Elephant Jello," "Electric Meat,"
"Microphone Saliva," i.e., word associations with a
key word.

Of the list of 20 put:
 3 stars for 3 best
 1 star more for two best
 1 star more for best best – i.e., 5 stars for the top
 banana

Take class vote among choice of the 3 best, compare
with subjective choice of the poet.

9) From above, form 17-syllable American Sentence
(regular subject verb object) from favorite oxymoronic
phrase. As:

"Bearded robots drink from Uranium coffee cups on
   Saturn's ring"
"The next speaker got nauseous swallowing Hitler's
   microphone saliva."
"The midget albino entered the hairy limousine to
   peepee."
"German farmers produced many tons of Nazi milk
   for the Führer."

10) Top ten epiphanous moments of lifetime: "Spots of
    Time," most vivid recollections since childhood.
    See: *Mind Writing Slogans:*
         13. Ordinary Mind includes eternal perceptions.
         15. Notice what you notice.
         17. Observe what's vivid.
         18. Vividness is self-selecting.
         16. Catch yourself thinking

    See Wordsworth *Prelude* Book XII, V. 208–225
    "There are in our existence spots of time that with
    distinct preeminence retain a renovating virtue,
    whence … our minds are nourished and invisibly
    repaired … such moments are scattered everywhere,
    taking their date from our first childhood. I
    remember well that once …"

    Also see Wordsworth *Prelude* Book XIV, V. 11–62
    "A light upon the turf"

    So list top ten lifetime hot moments, epiphanies,
       moments of experience.
    Can do it newspaper style: Headline, sub-head, lead
       paragraph, body of story, who, what, when, where,
       why.

11) Of these top ten: Take one and write one extended
    anecdotal narrative poem.

    Examples:
    Reznikoff's family anecdotes
    Marie Syrkin's "Finality"
    Wordsworth's *Prelude* Book XIV 1. 11–16,
    "A light upon the turf"

12) List top ten secrets you never told anybody. It may be
    embarrassing moments, crises, what makes you shudder

to remember to yourself, top ten shames, or secret
pleasures, minor discoveries, etc.

See: *Mind Writing Slogans:*
>   20. If we don't show anyone we're free to write
>   anything.
>   2. "Take a friendly attitude towards your
>   thoughts."
>   18. Vividness is self-selecting.
>   21. "My mind is open to itself."
>   22. "Each on his bed spoke to himself alone,
>   making no sound."

also see:
>   Atisa: "Abandon any hope of fruition"
>   A. G.: "Immortality comes later."

13) Of these top ten, take one, write an extended anecdotal
narrative poem.

14) List top ten fears, recurrent bad images of suffering,
that haven't yet happened.

Re: Atisa: "Always meditate on whatever provokes
resentment" in *Mind Writing Slogans*

See: *Mind Writing Slogans:*
>   2. "Take a friendly attitude toward your
>   thoughts."

Example:
A U.S.-Tibetan Guru's fear of being caught in a
Dharmic financial scandal like the Xtian Jim and
Tammy Baker's personal misuse of funds.

15) List top ten pleasurable experiences of lifetime.

16) Of the above, take one & write an extended anecdotal
narrative poem.

17) Describe a:
> Mystical experience
> Aesthetic experience   } Different
> Illuminative experience   names
> Religious experience   Same
> Peak experience   substance
> Memorable, happy, joy, moment

by means of describing external phenomena observed at the time:

    a) where you were – place
    b) what date, season, hour of day – time
    c) what you saw outside of you – external coordinates
    d) what thought - words went thru yr head (short & factual) at the time
    e) what thoughts went thru yr head afterwards (short & factual)

18) Top ten wishes
    Top ten lies
    Top ten dreams
    See Kenneth Koch's *Wishes Lies Dreams* handbook

19) Rhymed Blues
    Take one sentence more or less ten syllables, rhyme the end word 2 times more (original rhyme echoing in your head automatically suggesting rhymes) – Then fill in the blanks between end rhymes, keeping to a regular syntax: 12-Bar Blues Form.

    "Sometimes I think that you're too sweet to die
    Sometimes I think that you're too sweet to die
    Other times I think you oughta be buried alive"
            – Richard "Rabbit" Brown,
            New Orleans, 1929

Homework Exercises

9) Stop in tracks once a day, take account of sky, ground & self, write 3 verses haiku.

10) Sit 5 minutes a day, & after, re-collect your thoughts.

11) Stop in middle of street or country, turn in 360° circle, write what you remember.

                                       3/30/95

THICH NHAT HANH

Interbeing

If you are a poet, you will see clearly that there is a cloud floating in this sheet of paper. Without a cloud, there will be no rain; without rain, the trees cannot grow; and without trees, we cannot make paper. The cloud is essential for the paper to exist. If the cloud is not here, the sheet of paper cannot be here either. So we can say that the cloud and the paper *inter-are*. "Interbeing" is a word that is not in the dictionary yet, but if we combine the prefix "inter-" with the verb "to be," we have a new verb, inter-be. Without a cloud, we cannot have paper, so we can say that the cloud and the sheet of paper *inter-are*.

If we look into this sheet of paper even more deeply, we can see the sunshine in it. If the sunshine is not there, the forest cannot grow. In fact, nothing can grow. Even we cannot grow without sunshine. And so, we know that the sunshine is also in this sheet of paper. The paper and the sunshine "inter-are." And if we continue to look, we can see the logger who cut the tree and brought it to the mill to be transformed into paper. And we see the wheat. We know that the logger cannot exist without his daily bread, and therefore the wheat that became his bread is also in this sheet of paper. And the logger's father and mother are in it too. When we look in this way, we see that without all these things, this sheet of paper cannot exist.

Looking even more deeply, we can see we are in it too. This is not difficult to see, because when we look at a sheet of paper, the sheet of paper is part of our perception. Your mind is in here and mine is also. So we can say that everything is in here with this sheet of paper. You cannot point out one thing that is not here – time, space, the earth, the rain, the minerals in the soil, the sunshine, the cloud, the river, the heat. Everything coexists with this sheet of paper. That is why I think the word inter-be should be in the dictionary. "To be" is to inter-be. You cannot just *be* by yourself alone. You have to inter-be with every other thing. This sheet of paper is, because everything else is.

Suppose we try to return one of the elements to its source. Suppose we return the sunshine to the sun. Do you think that the sheet of paper will be possible? No, without sunshine nothing can be. And if we return the logger to his mother, then we have no sheet of paper either. The fact is that this sheet of paper is made up only of "non-paper elements." And if we return these non-paper elements to their sources, then there can be no paper at all. Without "non-paper elements," like mind, logger, sunshine and so on, there will be no paper. As thin as this sheet of paper is, it contains everything in the universe in it.

Excerpted from The Heart of Understanding:
Commentaries on the Prajñaparamita
Heart Sutra *by Thich Nhat Hanh.*
Reprinted by permission of Parallax Press.

ABOUT THE CONTRIBUTORS

Everybody is in
the act
from the point of view of Universality.
– Jack Kerouac

Each one is one.
There are many of them.
– Gertrude Stein

KEITH ABBOTT
Poet-painter-calligrapher Keith Abbott has published four novels, six short story collections, one memoir, and eleven books of poetry. His work has been translated into German, Russian, French, Italian, and Czech. He currently teaches at The Naropa Institute.

ROBERT AITKEN
Robert Aitken is the founder and retired director of the Diamond Sangha, a Zen Buddhist community in Honolulu. He serves on the International Advisory Board of the Buddhist Peace Fellowship. A former student of R. H. Blyth, he has authored and edited several books, including *A Zen Wave,* on Basho's haiku and Zen, already an enduring classic in the field. He has also given the West a strong sense of Zen ethics.

LAURIE ANDERSON
Multimedia performance artist and musician Laurie Anderson has recorded a number of albums, a CD-Rom, and one feature film. For her, "... image making and music are a form of meditation. ... I can sit 12 hours straight, not as a Buddhist but as a musician. I'm always looking for images and trying to imagine another way to view the world.

"I suppose the thing that attracts me the most to Buddhism is the sense of freedom," she says, "and that's also why I'm an artist: it's one of the few things you can do where you're free. I particularly relate to the nonauthoritarian aspect of Tibetan Buddhism and the emphasis on the ability of every single person to become perfect.

"In the current scenario, the Government becomes like the big father figure and often the artists are seen as the kids who should just sit down and shut up, and I think that's dangerous. The Buddhist concept of personal freedom is completely attractive: question authority, use your mind, make your own mind up. Of course, these have all been the watchwords of the avant-garde as well. As the country becomes more conformist, those ideas are getting lost."

TENSHIN REB ANDERSON
Tenshin Reb Anderson left advanced study in mathematics and Western psychology to practice Zen with Shunryu Suzuki, who ordained him as a priest

in 1970 and gave him the name Tenshin Zenki ("Naturally Real, the Whole Works"). From 1986–95 he was Abbot of the San Francisco Zen Center. He is currently Senior Dharma Teacher. He is author of *Warm Smiles from Cold Mountains,* a collection of talks on Zen meditation, and *Being Upright: The Unity of the Bodhisattva Precepts & Zen Meditation.*

ANONYMOUS TIBETAN NUNS

In June, 1993, some Tibetans in Lhasa arranged for a tape recorder to be smuggled into Drapchi, the prison where between thirty and forty Tibetan nuns were serving sentences of up to seven years each for having taken part in brief demonstrations calling for independence. Fourteen of the women prisoners recorded a number of songs, mainly laments addressed to their parents and relatives, or songs of praise for their exiled leader, His Holiness the Dalai Lama. The women sing of their determination not to give up hope for independence, despite their prison sentences. The tape was smuggled back out of the prison and copies were circulated amongst the underground movement in Lhasa. The authorities discovered the songs and, in October 1993, the fourteen women were re-sentenced by a Lhasa court and given additional sentences of up to nine years each for singing the songs. The women are still in Drapchi prison. To find out about Tibetan nuns in exile, contact the Tibetan Nuns Project, P.O. Box 374, San Geronimo, CA 94963.

BROTHER ANTHONY OF TAIZÉ

Brother Anthony of Taizé has translated modern poetry for many years. Besides the work of Ko Un, he has published translations of Kwang-kyu Kim and Ku Sang. He is the chairman of the English Department of Sogang University, in Seoul.

ANTLER

Antler is the author of *Factory, Last Words,* and *Ever-Expanding Wilderness.* He is a recipient of the Walt Whitman Award, a Witter Bynner Foundation Fellowship, and the Pushcart Prize.

SARAH ARSONE

Investigative journalist/poet Sarah Arsone is author of *Zen & the Art of Changing Diapers* and *Guilty.*

PETER BAILEY

Artist-calligrapher-poet Peter Bailey (1924–1991) revolutionized graphic design in the sixties. Among his last words were "I love everyone."

ANITA BARROWS

Anita Barrows is a prize-winning poet and a clinical psychologist. She has recently translated Rilke's *Book of Hours* with Joanna Macy.

JOHN CAGE

Composer John Cage (1912–1992) cast one of the widest aesthetic nets into the wild waters of the twentieth century. He published numerous books and graphic works as well as musical compositions, and was musical advisor for the Merce Cunningham Dance Company.

AMY CHAMP

Postmodern pilgrim, anthropologist, and performance poet Amy Champ currently resides in Williamsburg, New York, and works at the Japan-U.S.

Partnership for the Performing Arts. *Vote for Sun* is a video cabaret travelogue based on her journey to Zimbabwe, working with the Chembira Women's Theatre Group, and explores reality, politics, identity, and edges.

CHÖGYAM TRUNGPA

Of Chögyam Trungpa (1940–1987), Rick Fields said, "He caused more trouble and did more good than anybody I've ever known." He inspired the founding of Shambhala Publications, America's largest independent publisher of Buddhist texts. He once told Allen Ginsberg: "For Buddhists to speak of liberation of mind in America, they'd have to be poets," empowering him to establish a Poetics Department at The Naropa Institute, Boulder, Colorado, (codirected with Anne Waldman). Besides his autobiography, *Born in Tibet,* he is author of numerous books, including *The Path Is the Goal* and *Cutting through Spiritual Materialism.*

DAN CLURMAN

Dan Clurman is coauthor of *Conversations with Critical Thinkers* and *Money Disagreements: How To Talk About Them.* He tells us, "Writing poetry summons the mystery of the moment. An unknown voice surfs on sights, sounds, and memories. I listen. Words meander onto the page, revealing their delicious cargo, and once again, a messenger from Being Alive arrives as a poem."

JIM COHN

Jim Cohn's books include *Prairie Falcon* and *Grasslands;* spoken word discs include *Walking Thru Hell Gazing at Flowers* and *The Road.* He is founder of the National Deaf Poetry Conference and of the Museum of American Poetry, Boulder, Colorado.

JUDYTH COLLIN

Judyth Collin, "… upon being asked at a party if she was is a poet, and therefore is was she neurotic, mishearing it as erotic, cannot even possibly begin to explain herself, is fond of runaway chickens in Illinois, has fallen out of love with syntax."

CLARK COOLIDGE

Clark Coolidge is the author of *The Crystal Text, Heart of the Breath: Poems 1979-92, Own Face,* and *The Lowell Connector: Lines & Shots from Kerouac's Town,* and others.

GILLIAN COOTE

Gillian Coote is a Sydney-based independent filmmaker, writer, teacher, and student at the Sydney Zen Centre.

CID CORMAN

Cid Corman is author of more than eighty collections of poems, essays, and translations. Of himself, he writes, "Harvesting the sun / and earth and sky – no need to / gild the dragonfly."

PETER COYOTE

Peter Coyote "came from nowhere and is working his way back." Actor-writer-director, San Francisco Mime Troupe. Cofounder, San Francisco Diggers. Chairman, California State Arts Council, 1975–83. Since 1980, he has acted in over fifty feature films, such as *Jagged Edge, Bitter Moon,* and

Sphere, and narrated numerous documentaries. He is author of a memoir, *Sleeping Where I Fall.*

LISA CULLEN
Lisa Cullen writes: "Two women are waiting on a packed train platform in Calcutta. One of the women is hunched over reading *The Spiral Dance.* The other is absorbed in biting her fingernails. A cow ambles by. A rickshaw driver is arguing with a naked saddhu. A Tibetan woman is selling bone malas.

"Which character am I?"

THULANI DAVIS
Thulani Davis is author of the novels *1959* and *Maker of Saints,* librettist for Anthony Davis' operas *X* and *Amistad,* and is a Dharma teacher.

ATANU DEY
Of himself, Atanu Dey writes: "A thirty-something male living in California. Exploring metaphysics based on proper understanding of Physics. Currently devoted full time to finding out the answers to the more interesting questions about the universe – like why something exists instead of nothing, why mind appears to be of a different nature than matter, etc. Investigations of these questions appear to be far more challenging than being a product marketing engineer, as I used to be a few years ago."

DIANE DI PRIMA
Diane di Prima is the author of more than thirty books of poetry and prose, which have been translated into thirteen languages. Born in New York in the 1930s, she was active in the Beat movement. She moved to the West Coast in 1968, and currently lives in San Francisco, where she works as a writer, teacher, and healer, and studies alchemy and Tibetan Buddhism. Her most recent books are *Pieces of a Song: Selected Poems* (City Lights, San Francisco) and *Seminary Poems* (Floating Island, Point Reyes). An expanded edition of her epic poem, *Loba,* will be published by Penguin in May 1998, and Viking Press will release the first volume of her autobiography, *Recollections of My Life as a Woman,* in fall 1999.

PATRICIA DONEGAN
Patricia Donegan is a poet whose work includes *Heralding the Milk Light, Without Warning, Hot Haiku,* and *Bone Poems.* For several years, she has studied and taught meditation, lived in Asia, and given poetry readings. She recently cotranslated *Chiyo-ni: Woman Haiku Master,* with Yoshie Ishibashi, on Japan's greatest woman haiku poet.

ROBERT DUNCAN
Robert Duncan (1919–1988) never wrote a poem he couldn't sing. Thus Lawrence Ferlinghetti says, "He had the finest ear this side of Dante." From the late seventies, he was part of the core faculty of the New College of California's poetics program. *Publishers Weekly* noted, "Robert Duncan was one of the true masters of contemporary American poetry. His oeuvre is by turns lyrical, experimental, archaic, visionary and political."

MARIANE BAGGERS ERIKSEN
Mariane Baggers Eriksen is a psychotherapist and healer. She lives in Elsinore, Denmark.

LAWRENCE FERLINGHETTI

Poet-translator-painter-publisher Lawrence Ferlinghetti is the first American poet read by millions in his own lifetime. His most popular book is *Coney Island of the Mind* and his most recent is *Far Rockaway of the Heart*. Few people are aware he founded the first bookstore in America dedicated to paperbacks, City Lights, which also pioneered the homey library atmosphere now used by chain book outlets. City Lights' publishing company was a major vehicle for the Beats – made famous during the obscenity trial over Allen Ginsberg's *Kaddish* – and continues to remain contemporary and vital. The best Ferlinghetti biography so far is by fellow poet Neeli Cherkovski.

RICK FIELDS

Rick Fields is editor-in-chief of *Yoga Journal,* author of *The Code of the Warrior* and *How the Swans Came to the Lake: A Narrative History of Buddhism in America;* coauthor of *Chop Wood, Carry Water;* and cotranslator of *The Turquoise Bee: Love Songs of the Sixth Dalai Lama.* His most recent book of poems is *Fuck You, Cancer & Other Poems.*

NORMAN FISCHER

Norman Fischer is a teacher at the San Francisco Zen Center. He is the author of six volumes of poetry and a memoir, *Jerusalem Moonlight.* He is married and the father of grown twin sons. Emceeing the Poetics of Emptiness gathering at Green Gulch Farm Zen center, 1985, he said, "I do not think we will have spectacular results or even terribly noticeable results. But very steadily and gradually and clearly I think it becomes more and more impossible not to think of our minds our bodies our hearts and our words as of a piece."

GARY GACH

Gary Gach has translated Chinese poetry with Professor C. H. Kwock. He cofounded Isthmus Press with Reverend J. Rutherford Willems. Over the past several dozens of years, he has written maybe one or two good haiku.

DAN GERBER

Author of over a dozen books, Dan Gerber lives, teaches, and practices in Fremont, Montana.

ALLEN GINSBERG

Allen Ginsberg (3:VI:26–5:IV:97) grew up in Paterson, New Jersey, son of a poet who taught English and a mother confined in mental hospitals. William Carlos Williams was his family doctor and gave him a taste for American speech "as she is spoke" and the unvarnished, direct perception of reality. While a student at Columbia, he met Jack Kerouac and William Burroughs, and in Berkeley introduced himself to Gary Snyder, figures who would later become the nexus of the Beats.

His radical (and always nonviolent) activism provided a bridge between the Beats of the fifties and the civil rights, anti-Vietnam/American war and student movements of the sixties. He personified the American postwar avant-garde and over the past forty years has brought poetry to the people more than any other American poet. ("Poetry's role is to provide spontaneous individual candor as distinct from manipulators and brainwash. ... It comes from the bottom of the heart, expresses what is known universally and privately and hardly ever acknowledged in public.") His work has always been informed by the search for liberation. Though the Buddha appears in his early work, he didn't begin serious practice until 1971, when he met Chögyam Trungpa. His last teacher was Gelek Rinpoche. A recent biography, by Michael Schumaker, was entitled *Dharma Lion*.

BERNARD TETSUGEN GLASSMAN
Bernard Tetsugen Glassman is Abbot of the Zen Community in New York. He is coauthor, with Rick Fields, of *Instructions to the Cook: A Zen Master's Lessons in Living a Life That Matters*.

JONATHAN GREENE
Jonathan Greene "lives deep in the woods on a river, but you can never get deep enough."

TOM GREENING
Tom Greening is a professor at Saybrook Graduate School, a psychotherapist, and editor of the Journal of Humanistic Psychology.

SUSAN GRIFFIN
Susan Griffin is author of the seminal *Woman & Nature*, as well as *The Eros of Everyday Life: Essays on Ecology, Gender and Society*, and *Pornography and Silence: Culture's Revolt Against Nature*. Her practice leans toward vipassana and Vietnamese Buddhism.

OK-KOO KANG GROSJEAN
Poet-essayist Ok-Koo Kang Grosjean is author of *A Hummingbird's Dance*, a collection of poems. She has also translated books by His Holiness the Dalai Lama, Krishnamurti, Gary Snyder, and Thich Nhat Hanh into Korean.

SAM HAMILL
Sam Hamill is an essayist, poet *(A Dragon in the Clouds, The Nootka Rose)*, translator from Greek, Latin, Chinese, and Japanese *(Endless River, Midnight Flute, Only Companion, The Sound of Water)* and, for the past twenty-five years, editor at Copper Canyon Press. He also teaches creative writing in schools and prisons. He came to Buddhism through the writings of Kenneth Rexroth.

BUTCH HANCOCK
Butch Hancock first practiced sitting … on an earth-moving tractor in Lubbock, Texas, where he talked to the crows, red-tailed hawks, and coyotes. Along with Jimmie Dale Gilmour and Steve Young, he represents a new breed of American country singer, breakaways not only from Nashville, but who're also unbuckling the Bible belt – open to Castañeda and Rumi as well as Christ. Collections of his music include *Eats Away the Night, Own and Own,* and *Own the Way Over Here*.

ALLISON HARRIS
Allison Harris wrote "Nothing Much" in the seventh grade, in Will Staple's poetry class, sponsored by California Poets in the Schools.

JIM HARRISON
Jim Harrison is author of *Legends of the Fall, Wolf,* and numerous other novels, essays, screenplays, and books of poetry.

JANE HIRSHFIELD
Translator *(The Ink Dark Moon: Love Poems by Ono No Komachi and*

Izumi Shikibu), anthologist *(Women in Praise of the Sacred),* poet *(Lives of the Heart)* and essayist *(Nine Gates),* Jane Hirshfield graduated from Princeton and did postgraduate work, as it were, at the San Francisco Zen Center, Tassajara Zen Mountain Center, and Green Gulch Farm in Northern California, receiving lay ordination in 1979.

She states, "For me, poetry, like Zen practice, is a path toward deeper and more life. There are ways to wake up into the actual texture of one's own existence, to widen it, to deepen and broaden it, and poetry is one of the things that does that. It connects the things I know intellectually, what I feel, what comes through the senses, history, sociology, politics, passions, Buddhist experience. It's the only place where that many kinds of thinking are joined."

GARRETT HONGO
Garrett Hongo is author of *The River of Heaven, Volcano: A Memoir of Hawaii,* and *Under Western Eyes: Personal Essays from Asian America.* He is editor of *The Open Boat: Poems from Asian America.*

bell hooks
Native of rural Kentucky, bell hooks is Distinguished Professor of English at City College in New York and author of over twenty-five books, most recently *Bone Black: Memories of Girlhood, Wounds of Passion: A Writing Life,* and *A Woman's Mourning Song.* She is one of America's foremost writers on empowerment in the realms of gender, race, and class.

PATRICIA Y. IKEDA
Patricia Y. Ikeda began Buddhist practice at the Zen Temple in Ann Arbor, Michigan. She has traveled widely to Buddhist centers in North America and South Korea. She lives in Oakland with her partner and son.

LAWSON FUSAO INADA
Lawson Fusao Inada's most recent books of poetry are *Legends from Camp* (1993) and *Drawing the Line* (1997). He is professor of English at Southern Oregon University, Ashland. His teacher is the Venerable Lama Chhoje Rinpoche, founder of Padma Shedrup Ling Dharma Center, Fairfax, California.

ROBINSON JEFFERS
Robinson Jeffers (1887–1962) raised a family on a treeless headland overlooking the Pacific Ocean, in a dwelling built with granite stones named Tor House, where he wrote the majority of his work. He once said, "It is curious that flower soft verse is sometimes harder than granite, tougher than a steel cable, more alive than life."

WENDY JOHNSON
Wendy Johnson has been gardening and practicing meditation at Green Gulch Farm in California since 1975. She is working on a book about meditation and gardening.

JORDAN JONES
Jordan Jones is editor of *Bakunin – For the Dead Anarchist Within All of Us.*

KYOZAN JOSHU
Kyozan Joshu came to America in 1962, and is the founder and abbot of

Rinzai-ji Zen Center, Los Angeles; Mt. Baldy Zen Center, Mt. Baldy, California; and Bodhi Mandala Zen Center, Jemez, New Mexico.

JAAN KAPLINSKI
Jaan Kaplinski is an Estonian poet very much in the Buddhist tradition. His most recent book in English is *The Wandering Border.*

ALLAN KAPROW
In the late fifties/early sixties, Allan Kaprow created the "happening" – a kind of populist spontaneous environmental performance art. He wrote: "Not satisfied with the suggestion through paint of our other senses, we shall utilize the specific substances of sight, sound, movement, people, odors, touch. Objects of every sort are materials for the new art: paint, chairs, food, electric and neon lights, smoke, water, old socks, a dog, movies, a thousand other things which will be discovered by the present generation of artists ..."

DAININ KATAGIRI
Dainin Katagiri (1928–1990) came to the United States in 1963 after training at Eiheiji Monastery and working with the Soto Propagation and Research Institute and then for the Soto Headquarters Office in Tokyo. He practiced and taught at the Zenshuji Soto Zen Mission in Los Angeles, later moving to the Sokoji Soto Zen mission and then to the San Francisco Zen Center, where he assisted Suzuki-roshi. In 1972 he became the first Abbot of the Minnesota Zen Meditation Center in Minneapolis. He is the author of *Returning to Silence* and *You Have to Say Something: Manifesting Zen Insight.*

BOB KAUFMAN
Bob Kaufman (1925–1986) was taken to synagogue on Saturdays by his German Jewish father and Mass on Sundays by his black Martinique Catholic mother, but even then had Buddhist leanings. He shipped out on the Merchant Marines, was an important activist there, during which time he sailed around the world nine times. He once said, "Yeah, I must live in a different world because I live in a world where everybody sees me as just being a black man, but I don't see myself that way so I obviously must be living in a different world." A lover of poetry and jazz, he riffed in ways that partook of both to open up a third dimension, in many ways presaging hiphop.

ROBERT KELLY
Robert Kelly, originally associated with the Deep Image school of poetry, is the prolific author of such books as *Mill of the Particulars* and *Red Actions.* He came to Buddhism in 1982 "as a way of compassionate participation in the world." He teaches at Bard College.

JACK KEROUAC
Jack Kerouac's life (1922–1969) is one of the most written-about of his generation. His literary career begins when, as he recalls, "I was just sitting in my room and it was snowing and it was time to go out to scrimmage, time to go out in the snow and the mud and bang yourself around. And then, suddenly, on the radio it started – Beethoven!

"I said, 'I'm going to be an artist. I'm not going to be a football player.' That's the night I didn't go to scrimmage. And I never went back to football, see?"

In 1950, he wrote, "I want to work in revelations, not just spin silly tales for money." He was struggling with *On the Road,* and Denver architect Ed White, who carried around a pad to sketch interesting buildings, suggested Kerouac do likewise. Kerouac did so – using words instead – and soon had written eight novels which he carried around, unpublished, in a duffel bag.

Ginsberg would later call Kerouac's intuitive, freeflow word sketches "spontaneous bop prosody." Kerouac called it "the rhythm of urgency." He wrote to Malcolm Cowley, 11:IX:55, "What a man most wishes to hide, revise, un-say, is precisely what Literature is waiting and bleeding for – Every doctor knows, every Prophet knows the convulsion of truth. Let the writer open his mouth and ... get said what is only recoverably said once in time the way it comes, for time is of the essence. ... But it's hard, it's paradoxical, i.e., it's taken me all my life to near to write what I actually think – by not thinking." He also quoted the *Surapama Sutra:* "... you must learn to answer questions spontaneously without recourse to discriminating thinking." And: "Buddha told his young cousin Ananda, 'I am going to ask you a question, and I want you to answer me sponta-neously, without presuppositions in your mind. Because,' he said, 'all the Buddhas of the past, present, and future have arrived at enlightenment by this very method. The spontaneity of their radiance.'" He has also said, "Come back in a million years and tell me if this is real."

JERRY KILBRIDE

Jerry Kilbride was a bartender for over thirty years: "Have shot glass will travel" could have been his motto before retirement, as he has roamed the world. He was an integral member of San Francisco's Small Press Traffic Writers' Workshop and has been writing haiku since getting hooked on the genre in 1978 while living in Honolulu. He attended the University of Eastern Washington's "Summer Writers' Workshop" at the Irish Writers' Centre, Dublin, August 1995 – very definitely "A Brief Shining Moment in Camelot"!

MAXINE HONG KINGSTON

On the strength of her first two books, *Woman Warrior* and *China Men,* Maxine Hong Kingston has been the most widely-read author on American campuses of the past decade. Her *Tripmaster Monkey – His Fake Book* was inspired by Tripitaka Tang, the monk who went with Monkey to fetch the sutras from India. She leads a mindfulness writing workshop for veterans and their families, some of whom are published herein. She writes: "It is my faith that through art we can understand traumatic events, find their meanings, and transform ourselves and our society. To inspire ourselves and our writing, we practice sitting meditation, walking meditation, eating meditation, and study Buddhist precepts. Each group of veterans who write together, and read and listen to one another's stories, becomes a sangha."

The original draft of her unpublished magnum opus about peace went up in smoke along with her home and all her belongings in the tragic Oakland hills blaze, an event partly reflected in some of her notebook entries herein. Look for *The Fourth Book of Peace,* as well as *Hawaii One Summer.*

WILLIAM KISTLER

William Kistler is author of six books of poetry, including *The Elizabeth Sequence, America February,* and *Poems of the Known World.* His work has appeared in *Antaeus, Harpers, New Directions, Poetry Flash, The American Poetry Review, The New Criterion,* and he has served on the boards of several arts organizations, including Poets & Writers, Inc. (President 1980-1985) and the National Poetry Series.

KO UN

Ko Un was born in 1933 in southwestern Korea. Two years after the outbreak of the Korean War, he became a Son Buddhist monk. (Son is the Korean equivalent of the Japanese word, Zen.) After attaining a high rank in monastic life, he returned to the world in 1960. After years of dark nihilism, he became one of the main spokespeople for writers and artists opposed to the dictatorial regimes of the seventies and eighties. Incarcerated from 1980 to 1982, following the Kwangju Democratic Movement, he conceived of an epic cycle of poems *(Ten Thousand Lives)* to include every person he had ever met. In recent years his work has been marked by Buddhism again. He now lives with his wife and daughter in a village two hours away from Seoul. He has published over a hundred volumes of poetry, essays, fiction, drama, and translations of Chinese works. English renditions of his poems include *Beyond Self* and *The Sound of My Waves.* His best-selling epic Buddhist novel, *The Garland Sutra,* has been translated into English by Brother Anthony and Young-Moo Kim.

YUSEF KOMUNYAKAA

Yusef Komunyakaa is the author of *Lost in the Bonewheel Factory, I Apologize for the Eyes in My Head, Copacetic,* and *Thieves of Paradise.* He served in Vietnam as correspondent and editor of *The Southern Cross.* He received the Bronze Star. He is now associate professor of English at Indiana University. He was awarded the Pulitzer Prize for his poetry in 1994.

RICHARD KOSTELANETZ

Richard Kostelanetz works as an author, editor, and anthologist. With Schirmer Books, he has written *The Fillmore East* and edited *The Portable Baker's Biographical Dictionary of Musicians.*

TAKEHISA KOSUGI

Takehisa Kosugi creates mixed-media sound performances and installations, making use of daily materials and electronic technology.

In 1960 he cofounded the "Group Ongaku" in Tokyo, for antimusical neo-dada performances. He has been music director of the Merce Cunningham Dance Company since 1995.

JOANNE KYGER

Joanne Kyger's biography, according to poet Tom Clark, goes something like this: "A 'Navy childhood.' Places like Peking, China – Pensacola, Florida – Bremerton, Washington – Lake Bluff, Illinois – Upper Darby, PA – then in her fourteenth year back to the Sunshine State, eight years in Santa Barbara. Attended the University of California at Santa Barbara but ended up one unit (Biological Science Lab) short of a degree.

"Flight to North Beach. A book of poems, *The Tapestry and the Web* (Four Seasons Foundation, 1965). Residence in Kyoto, Japan, India, and Europe, New York City, San Francisco two or three more times. Experimental TV work at KQED. Then dropout back to the Bois, Bodega Bay, and now Bolinas, an hour north of the Golden Gate."

Author of sixteen books of poetry, she has taught at the New College of California and The Naropa Institute.

WILLIAM R. LAFLEUR

William R. LaFleur is Professor of Japanese Studies at the University of Pennsylvania. He has translated Saigyô, a medieval monk (*Mirror for the Moon: Poems by Saigyô 1118–1190*, New Directions) and is the author of *The Karma of Words: Buddhism and the Literary Arts in Medieval Japan*, as well as other works. He is completing *Freaks and Philosophers: Minding the Body in Medieval Japan* (Zone Books).

WILLIAM LARSEN

William Larsen lives with his wife, daughter, and assorted animals (both domesticated and not) in the Sierra Nevada watershed. A Vietnam veteran and practicing psychotherapist, he has been deeply influenced by the teachings of Thich Nhat Hanh.

DENISE LASSAW-PALJOR

Denise Lassaw-Paljor writes: "There are so many stories to tell. So many roads taken from great cities to great wilderness, across green oceans and red continents, breathing in the colors of poetry and examining just what it means to be a human being with two hands and a mind. Impermanence makes the colors richer, love makes them weep. What an adventure life is! I could tell you I was born of artist parents, or that I follow a blue bird vision and create the road as I go. What does it matter? The wind is always blowing us apart."

ALAN CHONG LAU

Alan Chong Lau was born in 1948 and obtained his B.A. in art from the University of California at Santa Cruz in 1976 (his work is represented by the Francine Seders Gallery, Seattle). His *Songs for Jadina* won an American Book Award in 1980. He writes, "Since I work in an Asian produce market, a lot of my poems are based on my daily exposure to the produce and the people who come to shop. In poetry, I'm just like the lady who lifts up a leg of daikon and snaps it with her finger hoping to hear the right sound."

JAMES LAUGHLIN

James Laughlin (1914–1997) began publishing poetry and short stories while in his teens. As a twenty-two-year-old sophomore at Harvard, he founded New Directions Publishing Company (circa 1936), and published authors including Vladimir Nabokov, Tennessee Williams, William Carlos Williams, Ezra Pound, Henry Miller, Dylan Thomas, Kenneth Rexroth, and Gary Snyder. His own poetry – often written in strict, Roman, quantitative meters – is finally gaining the wider, lasting recognition it deserves.

TAIGEN DAN LEIGHTON

Taigen Dan Leighton is a Zen priest in the lineage of Shunryu Suzuki. He has practiced at the New York and San Francisco Zen Centers; was head monk at Tassajara Zen Mountain Center; and practiced for two years in Japan. He is cotranslator and editor of *Cultivating the Empty Field: The Silent Illumination of Zen Master Hongzhi*, *Dogen's Pure Standards for the Zen Community: A Translation of "Eihei Shingi,"* and *The Wholehearted Way: A Translation of Dogen's "Bendowa"* with Commentary by Uchiyama

Roshi; and is a cotranslator of *Moon in a Dewdrop: Writings of Zen Master Dogen*. Leighton currently teaches at the Green Gulch Farm Zen Center in Muir Beach, California, and at the Institute of Buddhist Studies of the Berkeley Graduate Theological Union.

RUSSELL LEONG

Russell Leong edits the University of California at Los Angeles' *Amerasia Journal* and is a contributing editor to *Tricycle: The Buddhist Review*. E-mail: <rleong@ucla.edu>.

PETER LEVITT

Peter Levitt is a poet who has also published essays, fiction, and translations from Chinese, Japanese, and Spanish. The poet John Logan referred to Peter as "one of the finest lyric poets of his generation," and Robert Creeley has said that Peter Levitt's writing "sounds the honor of our common dance." In 1989, Peter received the prestigious Lannan Foundation Literary Fellowship. A longtime Zen Buddhist, Peter is an active member of the community at the Zen Center of Sonoma Mountain. His two most recent books are *Bright Root, Dark Root* and *One Hundred Butterflies*.

DIANA LEVY

Diana Levy is a mask-maker and poet who lives in the Blue Mountains west of Sydney, Australia.

WENDY LEWIS

Kyoshin Wendy Lewis has been practicing at the San Francisco Zen Center since 1987, spent six years at Tassajara Zen Mountain Center, and was ordained as a priest in 1997.

BRIGID LOWRY

An Aries with a tattoo of an island, a palm tree, and a planet on her left shoulder, Brigid Lowry is a New Zealander who lives in Western Australia. Once a waitress, then a school teacher, "... now I am an ageing hippy who has published poetry, short fiction, and two books for young adults, about to begin writing an adult novel. I am a zen student in the Diamond Sangha tradition and my influences include the beach, the beats, beetroot, haiku, and a life rich in pain and joy."

DAIGAN LUECK

A 67-year-old Zen priest, Daigan Lueck lived at Tassajara Zen Mountain Center for many years. Currently he resides at Green Gulch Farm with his wife Arlene.

JACKSON MAC LOW

Jackson Mac Low has written multimedia performance pieces, sound poetry, plays, radio works, and essays, notably on his own work and John Cage's writings, including *Barnesbook: Four Poems Derived from Sentences by Djuna Barnes*, *Representative Works: 1938–1985*, and *Asymmetries 1–260*, the first section of a series of 501 performance poems.

TAIZAN MAEZUMI

Taizan Maezumi (1931–1995) was the warm, friendly abbot of the Zen Center of Los Angeles (ZCLA). After forty years in the West, he once said he didn't feel Japanese anymore. He established six Soto temples in the U.S. and

Europe and ordained sixty-eight priests. Bernard Tetsugen Glassman now succeeds him as the spiritual head of the White Plum Sangha.

MANZAN
Manzan (1635–1714) was a Japanese Zen master in the Rinzai lineage.

ALEX MARLOWE
Producer/songwriter Alex Marlowe started playing piano at age nine, and began composing music at age eleven. (His poem here was written when he was ten.) He has studied at the Berklee College of Music as well as with Ozzie Ahlers and Joe Henderson. Alex has worked with Tony Toni Tone, Money B, Souls of Mischief, Saafir, King Tech, Domino D, Motion Man, EC Scott, WOGz, Sherwood, Suzan, and Soul Kitchen and played keyboards on remixes for D'Angelo, Coolio, and Barrio Boyz. His production company, Marlowe Music, develops new acts.

DON MARTIN
Don Martin (1931–1989) made paintings with cloth and lacquer, and drawings by blotting, smearing, and scraping, always seeking the gift of the accident. He created the painting reproduced on the cover of this book.

EVE MERRIAM
Eve Merriam (1916–1992) published her first book, *Family Circle,* in 1946 and now has over seventy-five titles in print. Her main interests were poetry, women in society, and exploring language through word origins. Works include *What in the World?, Ten Rosy Roses,* and *The Inner City Mother Goose.* Her most recent book of poems is *Blackberry Ink.*

THOMAS MERTON
One of the most important American Roman Catholic writers of the twentieth century, Thomas Merton (1915–68) was a Trappist monk and a prolific writer on both contemplative and social themes. One of the first to interpret Eastern spirituality to the West, he drew interfaith connections between Christian and Zen mysticism and intuition. Such poems as Song for Nobody, If You Seek, O Sweet Irrational Worship, A Messenger from the Horizon, Night-Flowering Cactus, Love Winter When the Plant Says Nothing, and The Fall, all reflect Zen experience.

JAMIE MEYERHOFF
Jamie Meyerhoff was raised at Tassajara Zen Mountain Center. She was sixteen when she wrote these poems.

JESSAMYN MEYERHOFF
Jessamyn Meyerhoff was raised at Tassajara Zen Mountain Center. She was fourteen when she wrote these poems.

CZESLAW MILOSZ
One of Merton's correspondents was Czeslaw Milosz. After taking part in the underground resistance to the Nazi occupation of Poland, he was cultural attaché to postwar communist Poland. Defecting to the West in 1951, he became an American in 1960. Nobel laureate for literature, his works include *The Collected Poems* and *The Captive Mind.*

SAKYONG MIPHAM
Sakyong Mipham is the lineage holder of the Buddhist and Shambhala

meditation traditions brought from Tibet by his father, and teacher, Chögyam Trungpa. Born in 1962 and trained in cultural traditions from both Asia and the West, he is the leader of the international Shambhala community based in Halifax, Nova Scotia. His poetry continues the impromptu, oral doha style of his father. [Doha is a type of verse or song spontaneously composed by Vajrayana practitioners as an expression of their realization.]

STEPHEN MITCHELL

One of the foremost translators of his time, Stephen Mitchell has given us new renditions of the Bible, Rilke, Lao-tse, and others. He has also edited Master Seung Sahn, a bestiary, and *The Enlightened Heart*.

KENJI MIYAZAWA

His translator writes that Kenji Miyazawa (1896–1933) "... was born and lived most of his life in Iwate prefecture in northern Japan. This area, sometimes called the Tibet of Japan, is known for poverty, cold, and heavy winter snows. His poems are all from there.

"He was born and lived his life among the farmers: a schoolteacher and a Buddhist." In 1989, North Point Press published a collection of his poems: *A Future of Ice*.

JOHN MUELLER

John Mueller is director of the National Poetry Association.

THICH NHAT HANH

Thich Nhat Hanh is a poet, Zen master, and peace activist. He served as chair of the Buddhist Delegation to the Paris Peace Talks during the Vietnam War, and was nominated by Dr. Martin Luther King, Jr. for the Nobel Peace Prize. He is author of more than thirty books, including *Living Buddha Living Christ, Being Peace, Peace Is Every Step,* and *Call Me By My True Names: The Collected Poems of Thich Nhat Hanh*.

ETSUDO NISHIKAWA

Etsudo Nishikawa is head of ceremonies at Sojiji Temple on the Noto Peninsula, Japan. He is in the lineage of the Sanbo Kyodan ("Three Treasures") school of Zen, combining elements of Soto and Rinzai.

WES "SCOOP" NISKER

Wes "Scoop" Nisker is editor of the book *Crazy Wisdom* and coeditor of the magazine *Inquiring Mind*. As a pioneer of freeform radio, he'd sign off his daily newscasts in the sixties by adding, "Remember, if you didn't like today's news – go out and make some of your own." His latest book is a course in evolutionary intelligence: *You're Not Who You Think You Are*.

CAITLIN O'DONNELL

Caitlin O'Donnell was born January 17, 1989, at Alta Bates Hospital in Berkeley, California. She is now eight and a half years old.

MARY OLIVER

Pulitzer laureate Mary Oliver's poetry is grounded in and grows out of a tenacious relationship between self and the world of owls, hummingbirds, egrets, ponds, the sun, family, etc. Her works include *Blue Pastures, Dream Work, House of Light,* and *A Poetry Handbook*.

YOKO ONO

Yoko Ono is an artist and musician. *Grapefruit,* first published in Tokyo in 1964, contains numerous instructions for events and conceptual art works. Her next book, *Acorns,* first appeared on the World-Wide Web. The Museum of Modern Art, Oxford, England, recently sponsored a major touring exhibition, and a retrospective is being organized by the Whitney Museum of American Art, in New York. She is widely associated with John Lennon. Their joint peace demonstration, a "Bed-In," was a major media event of the sixties. However, art critic Peter Frank writes: "Well before she emerged into popular awareness as John Lennon's wife, Yoko Ono had established herself in vanguard art and music circles as one of the most daring, innovative and eccentric artist-performers of her time. As one of the founders of the Fluxus movement at the beginning of the 1960s, Ono helped identify and define the playful, subversive, visionary sensibility that has undergirded experimentation in all the arts ever since. Her poem-like verbal scores, her films, and her staged performances anticipated everything from minimalism to performance art, the furthest reaches of new cinema to the most extreme of Punk-New Wave music. Her performances made signal contributions to what Fluxus mastermind George Maciunas called 'neo-Haiku theater' and artist-historian Ken Friedman labelled 'Zen vaudeville.'

"With her Fluxus colleagues Ono has elevated the insubstantial to monumental status, allowing us to contemplate the magic of the ordinary, as well as to comprehend the ordinariness of the seemingly profound."

NGODUP PALJOR

"Secretary to Mountains" Ngodup Paljor (1947–1988) became a child monk in Dzonga, Western Tibet, to fulfill his mother's promise to Tara, the goddess of compassion. The son of farmers and yak herders, he studied the Dharma until the Chinese occupation of his homeland forced his family to flee to India. A Buddhist scholar and translator (Tibetan, Sanskrit, Hindi, Pali, Thai, English), his work brought him to Alaska, whose high snowy mountains reminded him of home, and where he founded the Alaska Tibet Committee and Khawachen (Snowland) Dharma Center. He incorporated Japanese Zen with his native Tibetan Buddhism, as well as a deep appreciation of the traditions of all primal peoples. His poems were written while drinking tea near noisy streams. He died in an accident while working as a longshoreman on the docks of Anchorage.

REBECCA RADNER

Rebecca Radner is a San Francisco writer, intuitive consultant, and student of Tibetan Buddhism. Her work has appeared in publications including *Tricycle, Inquiring Mind, Iowa Review,* and *California Quarterly.* She reviews books regularly for the *San Francisco Chronicle.* Her forthcoming book is a spiritual memoir.

NOVA RAY

Nova Ray writes: "I was raised at Tassajara Zen Mountain Center. Through that I have experienced many things that I'm sure I would not had my parents not become so interested in Buddhism. They met and married there. I go there as often as I can. The people that have influenced me are Norman Fischer, Thich Nhat Hanh, and Issan. ..." ("The Last Flower" was written at age sixteen.)

DAVID TOKUYU REID-MARR

David Tokuyu Reid-Marr runs his own landscaping business and is committed to preserving the wilderness, particularly in the San Jacinto Mountains of Southern California.

PAUL REPS

Paul Reps (1896–1990) was part of the Greenwich Village scene until he learned about Ramana Maharshi. He went to Maharshi's hermitage in Kashmir, where he transcribed *112 Ways of Centering,* from four millennia ago. Artist-author of *Zen Telegrams,* his compilation *Zen Flesh, Zen Bones* (1952) is a classic introduction and source book.

KENNETH REXROTH

Kenneth Rexroth (1905–1982) was a painter-poet-translator-essayist-teacher. His book *One Hundred Poems from the Chinese* and the poem "You killed him" were seminal to the Beat Movement. Among his works are *American Poetry in the Twentieth Century, The Burning Heart: Women Poets of Japan,* and *The Orchid Boat.*

M. C. RICHARDS

M. C. Richards is best known as the author of *Centering.* Of "Snow," she writes, "Why do I write about moths and call the poem 'Snow'? Snow is crystalline, mineral, inert. Moths are alive, fluttering, impelled. The snow melts in the sun, dies. Turns to water, symbol of life. In the swirling snow I see the realm of life, not with my sense but with what you might call my supersenses: supersensible life. Life seeking life, the sun. Seeking light. The cold seeking the warm. The instinct seeking its transformation. Physical weather as the image of the dance of life; the quest, even in the heart of winter; the glorious sun making us ecstatic to burn ourselves alive in its energy, to worship at the center."

AL ROBLES

Al Robles is a native San Franciscan, longtime resident of the Fillmore district, founding father of the Kearny Street Workshop, and historian of the manongs, the first major group of Filipinos to come to America. As a poetry teacher, he works in prisons as well as schools.

GARY ROSENTHAL

Gary Rosenthal is a poet and psychotherapist. He lives in the San Francisco Bay Area, where, for years, he also ran an off-shore charter fishing boat. Point Bonita Books published an extract from his forthcoming collection of poetry, *The Museum of the Lord of Shame.* This year he published a collection of love poems, *The You That Is Everywhere.*

MIRIAM SAGAN

Miriam Sagan is author of over a dozen books, including *The Art of Love, Pocahontas Discovers America,* and *True Body* (poetry); and *Coastal Lives* and *Black Rainbow* (novels); *Tracing Our Jewish Roots* (kids), and, with Robert Winson, *Dirty Laundry: 100 Days in a Zen Monastery.* She teaches writing in Santa Fe.

SEUNG SAHN

Seung Sahn became a Zen master at age twenty-two. Fourteen years later, he became the first Korean master to teach in the West. His books include *Bone of Space, Dropping Ashes on the Buddha,* and *Only Don't Know.*

ALBERT SAIJO

Albert Saijo was born in Los Angeles, interned during World War II, drove cross-country with Jack Kerouac in 1959, and now lives and thrives in Hawaii.

NANAO SAKAKI

Nanao ("seventh son") Sakaki was drafted into the Japanese Navy, where he sat in on last suppers for young kamikaze pilots, and even saw for himself and identified the hydrogen bomb-loaded B-29 airplane headed for Nagasaki on his radar screen. Like the other defeated soldiers of his generation, he returned to a devastated nation that held nothing for him. For fifteen years, he roamed Japan's back country, a self-taught scholar and artist. In the early sixties, he met Gary Snyder and Allen Ginsberg and began corresponding with them. In 1969, he came to America. He has since walked four continents, founded an intentional community on an island in the East China Sea, and continues writing.

STEVE SANFIELD

Steve Sanfield was raised and educated in New England and has traveled to the Mediterranean, North Africa, the Greek Islands, and Hollywood. In addition to several books of poetry, he's written numerous equally noteworthy books of folklore and children's tales *(The Adventures of High John the Conqueror, Bit by Bit, The Feather Merchants)*. In 1997, he became America's first full-time storyteller-in-residence.

In deference to the unique form of haiku, he calls some of his work "hoops," and quotes Black Elk: "... the Power of the world always worked in circles and everything tries to be round. In the old days when we were a strong and happy people, all our power came to us from the sacred hoop of the nation, and as long as the hoop was unbroken, the people flourished."

LESLIE SCALAPINO

Leslie Scalapino is the author of numerous books, the most recent being *The Front Matter,* and *Dead Souls* (Wesleyan). Other titles include *The Woman Who Could Read the Minds of Dogs, Considering How Exaggerated the Music Is,* and *Green & Black: Selected Writings.*

ANDREW SCHELLING

Poet-translator Andrew Schelling was born in Washington, D.C., and raised outside Boston. He's tramped Thoreau's countryside and crossed India a couple of times. He's worked as a baker, truckdriver, bookseller, and teacher. Author of numerous books, he's currently an associate director of the Jack Kerouac School of Disembodied Poetics at The Naropa Institute. During the 1980s, he studied at the Berkeley Zen Center and then with Bernard Tetsugen Glassman, Sensei.

TED SEXAUER

Ted Sexauer served eighteen months as a medic in Vietnam, 1969–1970, first with the 571st Medical Detachment (Helicopter Ambulance) and later with a line company of the 173rd Airborne Brigade. A member of Maxine Hong Kingston's Veteran Writers' Workshop and a student of Thich Nhat Hanh, he resides in Sonoma, California.

SOYEN SHAKU

Soyen Shaku, abbot of Emaku-ji and Kencho-ji, Kamakura, Japan, brought

Zen "live" to America at the first Parliament of World Religions. His 1913 book *Sermons from a Buddhist Abbot* has been republished as *Zen for Americans*. Among his pupils were D. T. Suzuki and Nyogen Senzaki.

MIEKO SHIOMI (CHIEKO)

Mieko Shiomi (Chieko) (b.1938) studied music at the Tokyo National University of Fine Arts and Music 1957–1961. In 1963 he started composing the event pieces printed here and joined Fluxus. Since then he has been working on music pieces, performances, visual poetry, and object poems.

GARY SNYDER

Gary Snyder was born 8:V:30. As a youth, he worked on his family's farm in the Pacific Northwest and seasonally in the woods. He did a B.A. in mythology at Reed College in 1951 and graduate studies in East Asian languages, at the University of California at Berkeley. He made his first trip to Japan in 1956, where he studied Zen texts in Kyoto. More trips to Japan from 1959–1968 followed, plus half a year in India. He won the Pulitzer Prize for Literature in 1975.

Since the 1970s, he and his family have homesteaded in the foothills of the Sierra Nevada Mountains, Shasta bioregion, in a combination of nineteenth- and twentieth- century technologies, wood stoves for heat—photovoltaic cells for electricity. Snyder has traveled widely, reading poetry, teaching Buddhist meditation, and working on environmental and community issues. Since 1986, he has been teaching in the Creative Writing and Nature & Culture departments at the University of California at Davis. He is a member of the American Academy of Arts and Letters and the American Academy of Arts and Sciences. His latest book, *Mountains and Rivers without End,* is the product of forty years' work.

WILL STAPLE

Will Staple is a founding member of the Ring of Bone Zendo. He lives and writes in the northern Sierra Nevada.

CHARLES STEIN

Charles Stein teaches at Bard College and is associated with both Tibetan and Zen Sanghas. His works include *The Hat Rack Tree: Selected Poems from Theforestforthetrees* and *Being = Space x Action: Searches for Freedom of Mind through Mathematics, Art & Mysticism.*

HESTER G. STORM

Hester G. Storm writes: "Out of a reverent sense of the unity of all things comes this attempt to interpret the 'Way' of the ancient Chinese sage and mystic in terms of modern American Negro culture."

Lao Tzu ("the Old Master") was a Chinese contemporary of Confucius (sixth century B.C.E.). In his old age, he vanished into the West, leaving behind him the *Tao Te Ching (Book of Tao),* whence the religion Taoism gets its name.

LUCIEN STRYK

Lucien Stryk's most recent books are *And Still Birds Sing: New and Collected Poems* and *Where We Are: Selected Poems and Zen Translating.*

ROBERT SUND

Robert Sund is the author of *Ish River*. His poems in this book were written in a river shack, built up on pilings, in the freshwater tidal marsh of the Skagit Estuary, Washington. He now lives in Anacortes, where he is completing a large collection of poems and translating Japanese literature.

MITSU SUZUKI

Mitsu Suzuki was born in Japan, and, at the age of twenty-two, married a reconnaissance soldier. They had a daughter before he was killed in action in China. Her reputation as a kindergarten teacher during World War II caused Shunryu Suzuki to ask her to restore the kindergarten of the Zen temple in Yaizu, where he was abbot. Nine years later, following the death of his wife, she married Shunryu and followed him to America after he became abbot of Soko-ji Temple in San Francisco. Following her husband's death, she taught the Japanese tea ceremony for twenty years at the San Francisco Zen Center.

SHUNRYU SUZUKI

Shunryu Suzuki (1905–1971) was a Japanese priest in the Soto Zen tradition, who came to San Francisco in 1958 to minister to the Japanese-American congregation of Soko-ji, a temple in Japantown. As more and more people joined him in meditation, the San Francisco Zen Center came into being and he was its first abbot. Under his tutelage, Zen Center grew into City Center (San Francisco), Green Gulch Farm (Marin), and Tassajara Zen Mountain Center (near Carmel Valley). A collection of his talks formed the seminal book *Zen Mind, Beginner's Mind.*

ARTHUR SZE

Arthur Sze is the author of five books of poetry: *Archipelago, River River, Dazzled, Two Ravens,* and *The Willow Wind.* Sze's work has been published in translation in Italy and China. The recipient of many prestigious awards and fellowships, he directs the Creative Writing Program at the Institute for American Indian Art.

SHINKICHI TAKAHASHI

Shinchiki Takahashi (1901–1987) was born in a fishing village in Japan. Mostly self-educated, he was a prolific writer. However, in the introduction to his book *Afterimages,* he wrote: "As a follower of the tradition of Zen, which is above verbalization, I must confess that I feel ashamed of writing poems and having collections of them published. My wish is that through books like this the world will awake to the Buddha's Truth. It is my belief that Buddhism will travel around the world until it buries its old bones in the ridges of the Himalayas."

KAZUAKI TANAHASHI

Kazuaki Tanahashi is a painter, writer, and environmental worker. His works include *Brush Mind, Enku: Sculptor of a Hundred Thousand Buddhas, Moon in a Dewdrop: Writings of Zen Master Dogen,* and *Essential Zen.* He teaches brushwork for retreats at the American School of Japanese Arts and Zen Mountain Monastery.

JOHN TARRANT

John Tarrant is a roshi in the Harada-Yasutani lineage of koan Zen, one of the Dharma heirs of Robert Aitken; practices depth psychology; and directs the California Diamond Sangha. Originally from Tasmania, he currently lives in Santa Rosa, California, with his wife and daughter.

TASSAJARA ZEN MOUNTAIN CENTER SANGHA
The Sangha at Tassajara Zen Mountain Center, located high in the Ventana Wilderness, was visited by Thich Nhat Hanh in the early eighties. At that time, he shared some gathas for everyday practice, and invited the Tassajara Sangha to compose some of its own.

CLAUDE ANSHIN THOMAS
Claude AnShin Thomas began Zen practice in 1961. Upon graduation from high school, he volunteered for duty in Vietnam, where he served as a helicopter Crew Chief from September 1966 to November 1967. During his service in Vietnam, he was shot down on five separate occasions and wounded. He was honorably discharged in August 1968.

A political and social activist, after working to end the war in Vietnam, he addressed the plight of many of his fellow veterans suffering from homelessness, drug addiction, unemployability, social isolation, social ostracism, and abnormally high rates of suicide, divorce, and imprisonment. He speaks and leads retreats on mindfulness practice, personal transformation, and reconciliation, and is the founder of the Zaltho Foundation, promoting peace and nonviolence. In 1995, he was ordained a Zen priest by Bernard Tetsugen Glassman. He has two books forthcoming from Parallax Press.

LORENZO THOMAS
Lorenzo Thomas was born in 1944 in Panama. He teaches and writes in Houston, Texas.

THICH TUE SY
Thich Tue Sy is a young scholar-monk in Saigon. He was arrested following the "liberation" of the South by the Socialist Republic in 1978 and held without charges until February 1980. He was arrested again in 1984 and held without charges until September 1988, when he and other clergy were brought before a show trial. He and another monk were accused of sedition, and sentenced to death. This was commuted to twenty years' imprisonment, in response to international protest. For further information regarding anti-Buddhist repression under the new communist regime and what you can do, contact Stephen Denney, c/o the Institute of East Asian Studies, University of California, Berkeley, CA 94720, U.S.A.

AMY UYEMATSU
Los Angeles native Amy Uyematsu is author of *Nights of Fire, Nights of Rain,* and *30 Miles from J-Town.*

DEREK WALCOTT
West Indian poet and playwright Derek Walcott is noted for works that explore the Caribbean cultural experience. Some of his works include *The Arkansas Testament, The Bounty,* and *Star Apple Kingdom.* He received the Nobel Prize for Literature in 1992.

ANNE WALDMAN
Anne Waldman is a poet, performer, teacher, translator, and editor, with over twenty books to her credit. Former director of the St. Mark's Poetry Project, she designs and directs The Naropa Institute's Department of Writing and

Poetics. She has been a Tibetan Buddhist practitioner since the 1960s, when she met Geshe Wangyal, and was initiated by her root (principal) guru, Chatrul Rinpoche, in Nepal.

GARY WARNER

Though he still considers himself a Yankee, Gary Warner lives in Birmingham, Alabama, with his wife, Carol, and two children. Employed as a network engineer, Gary naturally turned to the Internet when he wished to learn more about haiku. The haiku world of 1992 was a print world and the World-Wide Web was, as yet, unborn. From 1993 until 1995, Gary's *Dogwood Blossoms: An Online Journal of Haiku* attempted to help fill that void [http://glwarner. narrowgate.net].

WANG WEI

Of Wang Wei (669–761), calligrapher Tung Chi'i-ch'ang said, "Artists before Wang Wei's time didn't lack skill, but they couldn't transmit the spirit of a landscape. They were hindered by the dust of their senses." Zen Poet Su Tung-p'o called him "China's only truly great landscape artist." Though no originals of his paintings have survived, much of his poetry was about his paintings. Emperor Tai-tsung eulogized him as the greatest poet of his time [early T'ang dynasty].

SOJUN MEL WEITSMAN AND ZEN CENTER SANGHA

Senior Dharma Teacher Sojun Mel Weitsman began practicing Zen Buddhism in 1964 with Shunryu Suzuki. He founded the Berkeley Zendo in 1967 and received priest ordination in 1969. In 1984, he received Dharma transmission from Shunryu Suzuki's son, Hoitsu. In 1985, he was installed as abbot of the Berkeley Zen Center, and in 1988 was installed as co-abbot of the San Francisco Zen Center.

The San Francisco Zen Center was established by Shunryu Suzuki in 1959. There are now forty residents, with a larger extended Sangha.

LEW WELCH

Lew Welch (born 16:VIII:26) once wrote, "I am Leo, my mane is longer than the sun." His former wife, Magda Craig, adds, "He was the sun and he was the drunk in the gutter, and he was the father, and he was the worker at the docks, and he was the citizen, and he was the friend – you couldn't name the manifestations!"

He was born in Phoenix, and, after service in the air force, studied at Reed, where he became buddies with Gary Snyder and Philip Whalen.

Some consider him "a Beatnik's beatnik." He worked as a cab driver in San Francisco, then fisherman, longshoreman, and teacher, while working on his finely crafted poetry. In addition to his collected poems, *Ring of Bone,* he is author of *How I Work As a Poet* (essays), *I, Leo* (an unfinished novel), and *I Remain* (correspondence).

He is Dave Wain in Kerouac's *Big Sur.* Aram Saroyan wrote a remarkable biography of him: *Genesis Angels.*

In May 23, 1971, leaving a farewell note at Gary Snyder's house, he walked out into the foothills of the Sierras, carrying a revolver. No part of his body was ever found. He disappeared, truly Gone Beyond. As Snyder says, "grasping the beauty of that ecstatic Mutual Offering called the Food Chain."

MICHAEL WENGER

Michael Wenger has been practicing Zen Buddhism for twenty-five years and was ordained as a priest in 1994. He is dean of Buddhist Studies at the San Francisco Zen Center. He is author of *33 Fingers: A Collection of Modern American Koans*.

PHILIP WHALEN

Philip Whalen was born 20:X:23 in Portland and educated at Reed. His "Scenes from the Life of the Capital" is one of the most neglected important long poems of the twentieth century. He is an ordained Zen Buddhist priest and is abbot of the Hartford Street Zen Center in San Francisco's Castro district. His latest book is *Canoeing Up Cabarga Creek: Buddhist Poems*.

NINA WISE

Nina Wise is a performance artist, writer, and Dharma student. She is currently working on a book of stories, *Secrets like Green-feathered Birds*.

TELLY WONG

Telly Wong was born in New York's Chinatown and raised in Brooklyn. She writes, "I am currently in my second year at NYU majoring in dramatic writing. I plan to pursue both screenplay writing and playwrighting. Through my work, I want to give voice to the neglected and the ignored and to create social change in today's amoral society.

"Through Buddhism, I have learned to love even though the other person may not necessarily do the same."

ADAM YAUCH

Adam Yauch is a member of the hiphop band, the Beastie Boys, and was first exposed to Buddhism on his second trip to Nepal. He is founder of the Milarepa Fund, <http://www.milarepa.org>, based in San Francisco, dedicated to the promotion and preservation of universal compassion.

Noting that his song, "Bodhisattva Vow," adheres fairly closely to the traditional rendition of the vow, he hastens to add: "A lot of people have the misconception that taking the Bodhisattva Vow delays enlightenment until all other sentient beings attain enlightenment, and that is not really it. The Bodhisattva Vow means striving for enlightenment to better help all other sentient beings attain enlightenment. Being enlightened is the best way to benefit all other beings – from that place you're able to help more."

AL YOUNG

Al Young is author of *Conjugal Visits, Drowning in the Sea of Love: A Musical Memoir*, and *Heaven: Collected Poems 1956–1990*; and editor of *African-American Literature: A Brief Introduction and Anthology*.

YOUNG-MOO KIM

Young-Moo Kim is a translator of modern poetry, including the work of Ko Un. He is a professor in the English Department of Seoul National University and is the author of many critical essays on modern Korean literature. His first collection of poems was published in 1993.

PAULA YUP

Paula Yup's work has appeared in *Mid-American Review, Passages North, Black Buzzard Review, Earth's Daughters,* and other anthologies and journals.

ACKNOWLEDGMENTS

I am supported by a sea of love, and a few names thereof, among family, friends, and associates, must be singled out, inextricably bound up with this endeavor.

Thank you Thich Nhat Hanh and Sister Chân Không. Thank you Katagiri Roshi, who first taught me zazen. To Parallax Press, for publishing what you practice; you have given refuge to what was initially a homeless idea, nurtured, supported, and enlightened it – over the years – without ceasing to paddle, even as we forged the rapids. That goes doubly for Michelle Bernard and Maria Hirano, whose astute editing and un-flappable aplomb amid multiple deadlines each deserve a refreshing snowball from my blazing hearth. Green tea for Ayelet Maida. Judy Hardin, for taking me to the gates, and Ellen Peskin, for walking with me to the booth. Wendy Johnson, for the be(e)s. Jim Hartz for the brilliant suggestions; Norman Fischer, some of whose curriculum is echoed here; George Fox, for the bibliographic treasures; Jerome Rothenberg, for the pointer(s); Barbara Gates, Peter Hale, Bob Rosenthal, John Hendricks, and Zen Center; Dr. T. Matthew Ciolet (RSPAS, ANU), SFPL, NYPL, Prof Net; Mechanics' Institute Library and the Bancroft Library; the WELL denizens at the Wonderland conference for being real as well as virtual; and my literary representative, Scovil Chichak Galen.

Grateful acknowledgment is made to the authors and publishers who granted permission to excerpt and reprint copyrighted material in this book.

"billygoat watches me work …," "drop my new pen …," "the grief counselor …," "The Illusion Collector, Age 37," "our honest neighbor's rolled …," "a windy clear day …," and "what she thought was …" by Keith Abbot. Reprinted by permission of the author.

Gathas from *The Dragon that Never Sleeps: Verses for Zen Buddhist Practice* (Parallax Press) by Robert Aitken. Copyright © 1992 by Robert Aitken. Reprinted by permission of Parallax Press.

"Wild White Horses" from *Stories from the Nerve Bible* (HarperCollins) by Laurie Anderson. Copyright © 1994 by Laurie Anderson. Reprinted by permission of Original Artists/Laurie Anderson. Laurie Anderson's comments in her biographical information are excerpted from Dimitri Ehrlich's "Musicians Look East Again," the *New York Times*, May 28, 1995.

"To Bodhidharma" and "To My First Teacher" by Reb Anderson. Reprinted from *Wind Bell* XX 11, spring 1986. Reprinted by permission of the author.

"The fragrance of the lotus ...," "Looking through the window ...," and "My country wasn't sold, it was stolen ..." by anonymous Tibetan nuns. Reprinted by permission.

"American History in Context," "Trees Seen Now," and "One Breath" by Antler. Reprinted by permission of the author.

"Father's Song" is reprinted from *Zen & the Art of Changing Diapers* by Sarah Arsone. Copyright © 1993 by Sarah Arsone. Reprinted by permission of Sarah Arsone. To order this book, call: (310) 459-4373 ($8.95 per copy, $2.50 for shipping and handling).

"Don't" and "Practice" by Peter Bailey are reprinted from *Wind Bell* XXV: 2, fall 1991. Reprinted by permission of the Zen Center.

Excerpt from "The River That Mines" by Anita Barrows. Reprinted by permission of the author.

Excerpt from *45' for a Speaker* is reprinted from *Silence* (Wesleyan University Press) by John Cage. Copyright © 1961 by John Cage. Reprinted by permission of University Press of New England.

Excerpts from "Vote for Sun," a solo performance by Amy Champ at So Grand Studio, SoHo, New York City, November 1996. Reprinted by permission of the author.

"Haiku" by Chögyam Trungpa. Copyright © 1983 by Chögyam Trungpa. Reprinted from *First Thought Best Thought*, edited by David I. Rome. Reprinted by permission of Shambhala Publications.

Tom Clark's biographical information on Joanne Kyger is adapted from *The Tapestry and the Web* (Four Seasons Foundation) by Joanne Kyger.

"The Berkeley Marina at Dusk" and "To David" are reprinted from *Floating Upstream* by Dan Clurman. Copyright © 1996 by Dan Clurman. Reprinted by permission of Sunyata Press.

"Jemez Mountains Meditation" is reprinted from *Big Scream #33* by Jim Cohn. Copyright © 1995 by Jim Cohn. Reprinted by permission of *Big Scream #33*. "On Non-violence & Observation" is reprinted from *Grasslands* (Writers & Books, 1994). Reprinted by permission of the author.

"The Layman's Lament" by Judyth Collin is reprinted from *Mind Moon Circle, Journal of The Sydney Zen Centre,* autumn, 1991. Reprinted by permission of the author.

"by a I ...," "listene ...," and "ounce code orange ..." are reprinted from *Space* (Harper & Row, 1970) by Clark Coolidge. Reprinted by permission of the author.

Excerpt from the lecture "Arrangement" by Clark Coolidge is reprinted from *Talking Poetics from Naropa Institute: Annals of the Jack Kerouac School of Disembodied Poetics,* edited by Anne Waldman and Marilyn Webb. Copyright © 1978 by Anne Waldman and Marilyn Webb. Reprinted by permission of Shambhala Publications.

"Tenzo's Song" and "You" by Gillian Coote. Reprinted by permission of the author.

"Learn to live …" is reprinted from *How Now* (Brattleboro, VT: Longhouse) by Cid Corman. Reprinted by permission of the author.

"Do you think …" by Peter Coyote. Reprinted by permission of the author.

"Reasons To Meditate" by Lisa Cullen. Reprinted by permission of the author.

"Aria from X: 'I would not tell you …'" is reprinted from *X: The Life and Times of Malcolm X – An Opera in Three Acts* by Anthony Davis. Libretto copyright © 1992 by Thulani Davis. Reprinted by permission of Thulani Davis.

"The Buddha and I" by Atanu Dey. Reprinted from Alt.Buddha.Short.Fat.Guy (UseNet). Reprinted by permission of the author.

"after months of sitting …," "black & white cat …," and "the pine shadow falls on the tent wall …" reprinted from *Seminary Poems* (Floating Island). Copyright © 1991 by Diane di Prima. Reprinted by permission of the author. All rights reserved.
"Buddhist Ruminations," "I Fail as a Dharma Teacher," and "Three 'Dharma Poems'" by Diane di Prima. Reprinted by permission of the author. All rights reserved.

"Check Up," "Half Open," "Something Happened," and "Tonight …" are reprinted from *Without Warning* by Patricia Donegan. Copyright © 1990 by Patricia Donegan. Reprinted by permission of Parallax Press.

"For the Assignment of the Spirit" reprinted from *Wind Bell* XVI:1, winter 1978–79. Copyright © 1979 by Robert Duncan. Reprinted by permission of the Literary Estate of Robert Duncan.
"I have …" reprinted from *Wind Bell* XV: 1, summer 1976. Copyright © 1976 by Robert Duncan. Reprinted by permission of the Literary Estate of Robert Duncan.

"I dropped something. I picked it up …" by Mariane Baggers Eriksen. Reprinted from *The Mindfulness Bell.* Reprinted by permission of the author.

"At Kenneth Rexroth's" is reprinted from *Open Eye, Open Heart* by Lawrence Ferlinghetti. Copyright © 1973 by Lawrence Ferlinghetti. Reprinted by permission of New Directions Publishing Corporation.
"Ecolog" is reprinted from *Northwest Ecolog* (City Lights) by Lawrence Ferlinghetti. Copyright ©1978 by Lawrence Ferlinghetti. Reprinted by permission of the author.

"Millennium Cities" is reprinted from *Trash* (Rome: Studio S – Arte Contemporanea). Copyright © 1996 by Lawrence Ferlinghetti. Reprinted by permission of the author.

"The Very Short Sutra on the Meeting of the Buddha and the Goddess," by Rick Fields. Reprinted from *Buddhist Peace Fellowship Newsletter*, spring 1989. Reprinted by permission of the author.
Rick Fields' comment in Chögyam Trungpa's biographical information is from his chapbook, *Fuck You, Cancer & Other Poems* (A Crooked Cloud Project, 1997).

"A Model of the Universe" by Norman Fischer. First published in *Wind Bell* XII: 2, fall 1988. Reprinted by permission of the author.
"Sesshin Poem" by Norman Fischer. Reprinted by permission of the author.
Norman Fischer's remarks in his biographical information are taken from "The Poetics of Emptiness" issue of *Jimmy & Lucy's House of "K,"* January 9, 1989.

"Inflight" by Gary Gach. Reprinted by permission of the author.

"Afterwords" reprinted from *A Last Bridge Home* (Clark City Press) by Dan Gerber. Reprinted by permission of the author.

"Against red bark trunk ...," "Not a word! Not a word! ...," "Walking into King Sooper after Two-Week Retreat," and 'White sun up behind pines, ..." from "Cabin in the Rockies"; "Four skinheads ...," "Manhattan May Day Midnight," and "New Stanzas for 'Amazing Grace'" are reprinted from *Selected Poems 1947–1995* by Allen Ginsberg. Copyright © 1996 by Allen Ginsberg. Reprinted by permission of HarperCollins Publishers, Inc. and the Allen Ginsberg Trust.
"At 4:00 a.m. the two ..." and "Stood on the porch in ..." from *Autumn Wind*, a film by Iara Lee (NYC: Caipirinha Productions). Copyright © 1993 by Allen Ginsberg. Reprinted by permission of the Allen Ginsberg Trust.
Buddha drawing by Allen Ginsberg. Copyright © by Allen Ginsberg. Reprinted by permission of the Allen Ginsberg Trust.
"The gray-haired man ..." reprinted from *Cosmopolitan Greetings* by Allen Ginsberg. Copyright © 1992 by Allen Ginsberg. Reprinted by permission of HarperCollins Publishers, Inc. and the Allen Ginsberg Trust.
"Mind Writing Slogans" were first published in a limited edition by Limberlost (Boise, Idaho). Copyright © 1994 by Allen Ginsberg. Reprinted by permission of the Allen Ginsberg Trust.
"Mind Writing: Exercises in Poetic Candor" reprinted from *Whole Earth Review*. Copyright © 1995 by Allen Ginsberg. Reprinted by permission of the Allen Ginsberg Trust.
"The moon in the dewdrop is the real moon ...," is reprinted from *Shambhala Sun*, I:5. Copyright © 1993 by Allen Ginsberg. Reprinted by permission of the Allen Ginsberg Trust.
"Sitting crosslegged on a wooden floor ...," by Allen Ginsberg. Copyright © 1971 by Allen Ginsberg. Reprinted by permission of the Allen Ginsberg Trust.

"Ascending the Mountain" by Bernard Tetsugen Glassman is reprinted from *The Ten Directions* III: 2, summer/fall 1982. Reprinted by permission of the author.

"Hut Poem #1" and "Ruts" by Jonathan Greene. Reprinted by permission of the author.

"My Children Visit the Zendo" by Tom Greening. Reprinted from *The Ten Directions*. Reprinted by permission of the author.

"Born Into a World Knowing" and "Summer Night" are reprinted from *Bending Home* by Susan Griffin. Copyright © 1987 by Susan Griffin. Reprinted by permission of Copper Canyon Press, P.O. Box 271, Port Townsend, WA 98368.

"Garden," "Iris," "Were I a Flower," and "Wind" are reprinted from *A Hummingbird's Dance* by Ok-Koo Kang Grosjean. Copyright © 1994 by Ok-Koo Kang Grosjean. Reprinted by permission of Parallax Press.

"Wanting one good organic line, ..." is reprinted from *Destination Zero: Poems 1970–1995* (White Pine Press) by Sam Hamill. Reprinted by permission of the author.

"Circumstance" by Butch Hancock. Copyright © 1997 by Two Roads Music (BMI). Reprinted by permission of the author.
"My Mind's Got a Mind of Its Own" by Butch Hancock. Copyright © 1996 by Rainlight Music (ASCAP). Reprinted by permission of the author.

"Nothing Much" is reprinted from *Inquiring Mind* VII: 2, spring 1992. Copyright © 1992 by Allison Harris. Reprinted by permission of the author.

"Not here and now but now and here ..." excerpted from "After Ikkyu" by Jim Harrison. Copyright © 1996 by Jim Harrison. Reprinted from *After Ikkyu* by Jim Harrison. Reprinted by permission of Shambhala Publications.

"Each Step" is reprinted from *The October Palace* by Jane Hirshfield. Copyright © 1994 by Jane Hirshfield. Reprinted by permission of HarperCollins Publishers Inc.
"The Heart's Counting Knows Only One" and "The Adamantine Perfection of Desire" are reprinted from *The Lives of the Heart* by Jane Hirshfield. Copyright © 1997 by Jane Hirshfield. Reprinted by permission of HarperCollins Publishers Inc.

"Something Whispered in the *Shakuhachi*" is reprinted from *Yellow Light* (Wesleyan University Press) by Garrett Hongo. Copyright © 1982 by Garrett Hongo. Reprinted by permission of University Press of New England.

"as they bury the dead" is reprinted from *and there we wept* (Golemics, 1978) by bell hooks. Reprinted by permission of the author.

"Wild Iris" by Patricia Y. Ikeda is reprinted from *Premonitions: The Kaya Anthology of New Asian North American Poetry* (Kaya Productions, 1996) edited by Walter K. Lew. Reprinted by permission of the author.
"Wood" by Patricia Y. Ikeda is reprinted from *Models of the Universe: An Anthology of the Prose Poem*, (Field Editions), edited by Stuart Friebert and David Young. Copyright © 1995 by Patricia Y. Ikeda. Reprinted by permission of Oberlin College Press.

"Clearing," "In So Doing," "Just Made It," "Keep Quiet," "The List," and

"Pledge" (excerpted from "In So Doing"), "Forest Family" and "Ness" (excerpted from "The Journey South"), and "In/Vocation" are reprinted from *Legends from Camp* (Coffee House Press) by Lawson Fusao Inada. Copyright © 1993 by Lawson Fusao Inada. Reprinted by permission of Coffee House Press.

"A Nice Place" is reprinted from *Drawing the Line* (Coffee House Press) by Lawson Fusao Inada. Copyright © 1997 by Lawson Fusao Inada. Calligraphy by Michele Laporte from *Tricycle: The Buddhist Review* IV:3, spring 1995. Reprinted by permission of Michele Laporte and Coffee House Press.

"Carmel Point" is reprinted from *Rock and Hawk* by Robinson Jeffers. Copyright © 1929 and 1957 by Robinson Jeffers. Reprinted by permission of Random House, Inc. and Jeffers Literary Properties.

"River Meditation" by Wendy Johnson. Reprinted from *Wind Bell*, 1986. Reprinted by permission of the author.

"Zen Baker" by Jordan Jones. Reprinted by permission of the author.

"Whenever I hear …" by Kyozan Joshu. Translated from the Japanese by Greg Campbell and Jikan Leonard Cohen. Reprinted from *Metamorphosis*, winter 1997. Reprinted by permission.

"Once I got a postcard …" and "Shunryu Suzuki …" by Jaan Kaplinski. Copyright © 1987 by Jaan Kaplinski. Reprinted from *The Wandering Border* by Jaan Kaplinski, translated from the Estonian by the author, Sam Hamill, and Riina Tamm. Reprinted by permission of Sam Hamill and Copper Canyon Press, P.O. Box 271, Port Townsend, WA, 98368.

"Suppose you telephone your own answering …" by Allan Kaprow. Copyright © 1993 by Allan Kaprow. Reprinted from *Essays on the Blurring of Art & Life: Allan Kaprow*, edited and translated by Jeff Kelley. Reprinted by permission of the Regents of the University of California Press.
Allan Kaprow's statement in his biographical information is from his essay on Jackson Pollack.

"Peaceful Life" by Dainin Katagiri. Reprinted from *MZMC News*, XVI, 1, spring 1991. Reprinted by permission of Minnesota Zen Meditation Center.
"You are nearly as old as the number of years it has been …" is reprinted from *Wind Bell*, 1986. Reprinted by permission of Minnesota Zen Meditation Center.

"… solitary thoughts on death and other illegal mysteries …" (excerpted from "Does the Secret Mind Whisper?"), "… there is a silent beat in between the drums …" (excerpted from "Letter to the Editor," addendum to "O Jazz-O War Memoir: Jazz, Don't Listen to It at Your Own Risk"), and "THE TRIP, DHARMA TRIP, SANGHA TRIP" are reprinted from *Cranial Guitar: Selected Poems* (Coffee House Press) by Bob Kaufman, edited by Gerald Nicosia. Copyright © 1996 by Eileen Kaufman. Reprinted by permission of Coffee House Press.

Excerpts from *The Flowers of Unceasing Coincidence* (Talman Company) by Robert Kelly. Copyright © 1988 by Robert Kelly. Reprinted by permission of the author.

"Holy Sonnet" is reprinted from *Red Actions: Selected Poems, 1960–1993* by Robert Kelly. Reprinted by permission of Black Sparrow Press.

"Sermon on Language" by Robert Kelly. Reprinted by permission of the author.

"Bathtub Thought" is reprinted from *Pomes All Sizes* by Jack Kerouac. Copyright © 1992 by John Sampas, Literary Representative. Reprinted by permission of City Lights Books.

"Birds singing …," "The bottoms of my shoes …," "To Edward Dahlberg," "Missing a kick …," "The moon had …," and "In my medicine cabinet; …" are reprinted from *Scattered Poems* by Jack Kerouac. Copyright © 1971 by The Estate of Jack Kerouac. Reprinted by permission of City Lights Books.

Excerpts from *The Scripture of the Golden Eternity* (City Lights Books) by Jack Kerouac. Copyright © 1960 by Jack Kerouac. Reprinted by permission of Sterling Lord Literistic, Inc.

"Orizaba Blues: 64th Chorus," and "Orlanda Blues: 24th Chorus" from *The Book of Blues* (Penguin) by Jack Kerouac. Copyright © 1959 by the Estate of Stella Kerouac, John Sampas Literary Representative. Reprinted by permission of Sterling Lord Literistic, Inc.

Jack Kerouac's reminiscence about becoming an artist is reprinted from "The Beat Generation, Part II," by Al Aronowitz, *New York Post*, March 10, 1959. The other quotes are from *Jack Kerouac: Selected Letters, 1940–1956* (Viking, 1995) edited by Ann Charters.

"the cool surface …," "firecrackers, …," "the harpist …," "jumping rope …," "the nurse speaks of christmas …," "still in the taste …," and "the wheelchair child …" by Jerry Kilbride. Reprinted by permission of the author.

Excerpts from Maxine Hong Kingston's journals. Copyright © 1990 by Maxine Hong Kingston. Entries beginning "Suddenly free …" and "Thought about 3:15 a.m. …" are reprinted from *The Writer's Diary* (HarperCollins) edited by Howard Junker. Copyright © 1995. Reprinted by permission of the author.

"Kyoto I – Kinkaku-ji" and "Kyoto II – Ryoanji" by William Kistler. Reprinted by permission of the author.

"Standing near the Ghats Along the Ganges" is reprinted from *Notes Drawn from the River of Ecstasy* (San Francisco/Tulsa: Council Oak Books) by William Kistler. Copyright © 1997 by William Kistler. Reprinted by permission of the author.

"Annihilation" by Ko Un, translated by Young-Moo Kim and Brother Anthony. Reprinted by permission of the translators.

"Asking the Way," "Baby," "Ripples," and "Walking down a mountain" are reprinted from *Beyond Self* by Ko Un, translated by Young-Moo Kim and Brother Anthony. Copyright © 1997 by Ko Un. Reprinted by permission of Parallax Press.

"2527th Birthday of the Buddha" and "We Never Know" are reprinted from *Dien Cai Dau* (Wesleyan University Press) by Yusef Komunyakaa. Copyright © 1988 by Yusef Komunyakaa. Reprinted by permission of University Press of New England.

"A to Z" is reprinted by permission of Richard Kostelanetz. Copyright © 1994 by Richard Kostelanetz. (P.O. Box 444, Prince Street, New York, NY 10012). Reprinted by permission of the author.

"Anima 1," "Chironomy," "Manodharma with Mr. Y.," "Micro 1," "Organic Music," and "Theater Music" by Takehisa Kosugi. Reprinted from *Fluxus Editions*. Copyright © 1965 by Takehisa Kosugi. Reprinted by permission of the author.

"Bird family ...," "Never talk ahead ...," and "Oh Man is the highest type of animal existing ..." are reprinted from *Just Space: Poems 1979–1989* (Black Sparrow Press) by Joanne Kyger. Copyright © 1989 by Joanne Kyger. Reprinted by permission of the author.
"Dream," "The Empty Shrine Buddha," and "It's a great day ...," are reprinted from *Going On: Selected Poems 1958–1980* (Dutton). Copyright © 1983 by Joanne Kyger. Reprinted by permission of the author.
"Duncan's class met last night ..." is reprinted from *The Dharma Committee* (Smithereens Press). Copyright © 1986 by Joanne Kyger. Reprinted by permission of the author.

"Wedding Party" by William R. LaFleur is reprinted from *The Ten Directions* I:2, May 1980. Reprinted by permission of the author.

"Surrender" by William Larsen. Reprinted by permission of the author.

"Counting Breaths" and "For a Moose" by Denise Lassaw-Paljor. Reprinted by permission of the author.

"bittermelon," "morning reflections over the miso soup," and "wintermelon" by Alan Chong Lau. Reprinted by permission of the author. "eating habits of the old man" is reprinted from *Songs for Jadina* (Greenfield Review Press: Greenfield, NY 12833) by Alan Chong Lau. Copyright © 1980 by Alan Chong Lau. Reprinted by permission of the author.

"What Is Hoped for" by James Laughlin. Copyright © 1942 by James Laughlin. Reprinted by permission of the author.

"All of Us So Close to Buddha" and "Giving Buddha to all beings is giving to oneself. ..." by Taigen Dan Leighton. Reprinted by permission of the author.

"Threads" is reprinted from *Country of Dreams and Dust* (University of New Mexico, 1994) by Russell Leong. Reprinted by permission of the author.
"What Does the Body Dream at Rest?" by Russell Leong. Reprinted from *Tricycle: The Buddhist Review* VII:1, fall 1997. Reprinted by permission of the author.

Excerpts from *100 Butterflies* (Broken Moon Press) by Peter Levitt.

"a million times" "the resounding echo of the buddha's words," and "snow" by Jessemyn Meyerhoff. Reprinted by permission of the author.

"Gift" is reprinted from *The Collected Poems* by Czeslaw Milosz. Copyright © 1988 by Czeslaw Milosz Royalties, Inc. Reprinted by permission of The Ecco Press.

"Bamboo," "Orchid and Rock," and "The Sense of Proportion" are reprinted from *Parables and Portraits* by Stephen Mitchell. Copyright © 1990 by Stephen Mitchell. Reprinted by permission of HarperCollins Publishers Inc.

"Rubber Eraser" by John Mueller. Reprinted by permission of the author.

"Snow Fell Twice, the Sun Always Shone" is reprinted from *Smile of the Tiger* (Vajradhatu Publications) by Osel Rangdrol Mukpo. Copyright © 1998 by Mipham J. T. Mukpo. Reprinted by permission of Mipham J. T. Mukpo.

"Cars stuck in the snow ...," " "exhausted by jogging ...," "I woke up early ...," "Robert Frost and I ...," "The Way," and "The wish of my Amala ..." by Ngodup Paljor. Reprinted by permission of the Estate of Ngodup Paljor.

"Existence," "Journey," and "Please Call Me by My True Names" are reprinted from *Call Me by My True Names: The Collected Poems of Thich Nhat Hanh* by Thich Nhat Hanh. Copyright © 1993 by Thich Nhat Hanh. Reprinted by permission of Parallax Press.

"Round, round, more round than the moon; ..." by Etsudo Nishikawa. Reprinted from The *Ten Directions,* III: 2, summer/fall 1982. Reprinted by permission.

"No tears and no fears ..." and "Whatever" by Wes "Scoop" Nisker. Reprinted by permission of the author.

"Footprints" by Caitlin O'Donnell. Reprinted from *Inquiring Mind* VII:2, spring 1992. Reprinted by permission of the author.

"Going to Walden" is reprinted from *The River Styx, Ohio, and Other Poems* (Harcourt Brace Jovanovich) by Mary Oliver. Copyright © 1972 by Mary Oliver. Reprinted by permission of Molly Malone Cook Literary Agency.

"Painting to Be Constructed in Your Head," "Painting to Hammer a Nail," and "Smoke Painting" are reprinted from *Instruction Paintings* (Weatherhill) by Yoko Ono. Copyright © 1995 by Yoko Ono. Reprinted by permission of the artist.

"I Want to Write like a Postcard" and "Like That" by Rebecca Radner. Reprinted by permission of the author.

"The Last Flower" by Nova Ray. Reprinted by permission of the author.

"Cedar," "Condor," "Live Oak," and "Zen Mountain Center" by David Tokuya Reid Marr. Reprinted from *The Ten Directions,* fall/winter 1990. Reprinted by permission.

"Poems Before Words" are reprinted from *Sit In: What It Is Like* by Paul Reps. Copyright © 1975 by Paul Reps. Reprinted by permission of Zen Center Press.

"Void Only" is reprinted from *Flower Wreath Hill* by Kenneth Rexroth. Copyright © 1979 by Kenneth Rexroth. Reprinted by permission of New Directions Publishing Corporation.
"Water is always the same ..." is excerpted from "The Heart's Garden, The Garden's Heart," reprinted from *The Collected Longer Poems of Kenneth Rexroth* by Kenneth Rexroth. Copyright © 1967 by Kenneth Rexroth. Reprinted by permission of New Directions Publishing Corporation.

"Snow" is reprinted from *Centering in Pottery, Poetry, & the Person* by M. C. Richards. Copyright © 1989 by M. C. Richards. Reprinted by permission of Wesleyan University Press.
M. C. Richards' commentary on her work in her biographical information is from the same source.

"Ryokan the Crazy Snow Poet" is reprinted from *Rappin' with 10,000 Carabaos in the Dark* by Al Robles. Copyright © 1996 by Al Robles. Reprinted by permission of the University of California at Los Angeles Asian American Studies Center.

"Ghetto Dokusan" is reprinted from *The Museum of the Lord of Shame* by Gary Rosenthal. Copyright © 1997 by Gary Rosenthal. Reprinted by permission of Point Bonita Books.
"Wild Hooves" is reprinted from *The You That Is Everywhere* by Gary Rosenthal. Copyright © 1997 by Gary Rosenthal. Reprinted by permission of Point Bonita Books.

"Winter burn" is reprinted from *True Body* by Miriam Sagan. Copyright © 1991 by Miriam Sagan. Reprinted by permission of Parallax Press.

"Good and Bad are eminent teachers ..." and "The mountain sinks into the sea ..." are reprinted from *Bone of Space: Poems by Zen Master Seung Sahn* by Seung Sahn. Copyright © 1984, 1993 by Seung Sahn. Reprinted by permission of Primary Point Press.

"Bodhisattva Vows" is reprinted from *OUTSPEAKS A RHAPSODY* (Honolulu: Bamboo Ridge Press) by Albert Saijo. Copyright © 1997 by Albert Saijo. Reprinted by permission of the author.

"If you have time to chatter ...," "Just Enough," "North America," "Sugar Loaf Hill," and "Top Ten of American Poetry" are reprinted from *Break the Mirror: Poems by Nanao Sakaki* (Nobleboro, ME: Blackberry Books) by Nanao Sakaki. Copyright © 1995 by Nanao Sakaki. Reprinted by permission of Blackberry Books.
"Let's Eat Stars" is reprinted from *Let's Eat Stars* (Nobleboro, ME: Blackberry Books) by Nanao Sakaki. Copyright © 1997 by Nanao Sakaki. Reprinted by permission of Blackberry Books.

"Alone in the house ...," "Birthday Poem," "Hills of buttercups ...," and "Walking in the rain ..." are reprinted from *Backlog* (Guadalupita, NM: Tooth of Time, 1975) by Steve Sanfield. Reprinted by permission of the author.

"Concern," "I like my poems short …," and "A Poem for Those of You Who Are Sometimes Troubled by Barking Dogs and Low Flying Jets" by Steve Sanfield are reprinted from *American Zen: By a Guy Who Tried It* (Monterey, KY: Larkspur Press, 1994) Reprinted by permission of the author.

"A man getting on a bus …" by Leslie Scalapino. Reprinted by permission of the author.

"Run My Hand Under" is reprinted from *Old Growth: Selected Poems and Notebooks, 1986–1994* (Rodent Press) by Andrew Schelling. Copyright © by Andrew Schelling. Reprinted by permission of the author.

"The Ambivalent Nature of Healing" and "Poem for Têt" by Ted Sexauer. Reprinted by permission of the author.
"The Well" is reprinted from *Turning Wheel: Journal of the Buddhist Peace Fellowship,* spring, 1995. Reprinted by permission of the author.

"En Route to America" by Soyen Shaku. Reprinted from *How the Swans Came to the Lake: A Narrative History of Buddhism in America* (Shambhala) by Rick Fields. Copyright © 1981 by Rick Fields. Reprinted by permission.

"Disappearing Music for Face," "Event for Late Afternoon," "Mirror," "Music for Two Players II," "Passing Music for a Tree," and "Portrait Piece" reprinted from *Fluxus Editions.* Copyright © 1963, 1964 by Mieko Shiomi (Chieko). Reprinted by permission of Mieko Shiomi (Chieko).

"As for Poets," "Avocado," and "Without" are reprinted from *Turtle Island.* Copyright © 1974 by Gary Snyder. Reprinted by permission of New Directions Publishing Corporation.
"Earth Verse" is reprinted from *Mountains and Rivers Without End* (Counterpoint). Copyright © 1996 by Gary Snyder. Reprinted by permission of Counterpoint Press.
"How Poetry Comes to Me," is reprinted from *No Nature* (Pantheon). Copyright © 1992 by Gary Snyder. Reprinted by permission of Pantheon Books, a division of Random House, Inc.
"Saying Farewell at the Monastery after Hearing the Old Master Lecture on 'Return to the Source,'" is reprinted from *Left Out in the Rain* (North Point Press). Copyright © 1986 by Gary Snyder. Reprinted by permission of Farrar Straus & Giroux.
"Smokey the Bear Sutra" by Gary Snyder. Reprinted by permission of Gary Snyder.
"Song of the Taste" is reprinted from *Regarding Wave.* Copyright © 1970 by Gary Snyder. Reprinted by permission of New Directions Publishing Corporation.

"Shen Tao" is reprinted from *Passes for Human* (Berkeley: Shaman's Drum, 1976) by Will Staple. Reprinted by permission of the author.

"My hat vanished …" is reprinted from *The Hat Rack Tree: Selected Poems from Theforestforthetrees* (Station Hill, 1994) by Charles Stein. Reprinted by permission of the author.

"Bop for Laotzu" is reprinted from *Bop for Laotzu and Other American Versions of Chinese Poetry* (Golden Mountain Press, 1962) by Hester G. Storm.

"The Frog I Saved from a Snake" and "Two Poems for the Good Given" are reprinted from *Shack Medicine* (The Poet's House Press) by Robert Sund. Copyright © 1990, 1992 by Robert Sund. Reprinted by permission of the author.

The quotation by D. T. Suzuki used in Gary Gach's preface is reprinted from *Mysticism: Christian and Buddhist* by Daisetz Teitaro Suzuki (Harper and Company). Copyright © 1957 by D. T. Suzuki.

All selections by Mitsu Suzuki are reprinted from *Temple Dusk* by Mitsu Suzuki. Copyright © 1992 by Mitsu Suzuki. Reprinted by permission of Parallax Press.

"Beginner's Mind" is reprinted from *Zen Mind, Beginner's Mind* (Weatherhill) by Shunryu Suzuki. Copyright © 1970 by Shunryu Suzuki. Reprinted by permission of Zen Center (San Francisco) and Weatherhill.

"Fauve," "Ice Floe," and "The Silence" are reprinted from *The Redshifting Web: Poems 1970 – 1998* (Copper Canyon Press) by Arthur Sze. Reprinted by permission of Copper Canyon Press, P.O. Box 271, Port Townsend, WA, 98368.

"Words" by Shinkichi Takahashi, translated by Lucien Stryk and Takashi Ikemoto. Reprinted from *Zen Poetry: Let the Spring Breeze Enter* by Shinkichi Takahashi. Copyright © 1995 by Shinkichi Takahashi. Reprinted by permission of Grove Press.
Takahashi's quotation in his biographical information is from the same source.

"Can five hundred paintings be created in one stroke?," "Does the brush paint, or does the ink? Or does the paper, ...," and "One-line poem? Why not one-word poem?" by Kazuaki Tanahashi are reprinted from *Brush Mind*. Copyright © 1990 by Kazuaki Tanahashi. Reprinted by permission of Parallax Press.
Six characters from the *Heart Sutra* from *Wind Bell,* fall 1989. Reprinted by permission of Kazuaki Tanahashi.

"Han Shan in Santa Rosa" by John Tarrant. Reprinted from *Dharma Family Treasures: Sharing Mindfulness with Children,* edited by Sandy Eastoak. Copyright © 1994 by Sandy Eastoak. Reprinted by permission of North Atlantic Books.
"The Hula Dancers Dance the Hula, Kilauea the Caldera" is reprinted from *Blind Donkey*. Reprinted by permission of the author.

Gathas by monks and students of Tassajara Zen Mountain Center. Reprinted by permission of Zen Center.

"A / bullet / slams ...," "Alone / with only ...," "Anyone can ...," and *"As / the / soldiers ... "* by Claude AnShin Thomas. Reprinted by permission of the author.

"MMDCCXIII ½" is reprinted from *Chances are Few* (Blue Wind Press, 1979) by Lorenzo Thomas. Reprinted by permission of Blue Wind Press and Lorenzo Thomas.

"A Cup of Clear Water," "Hermit Thoughts," and "Stone Walls," translated by Trevor Carolan and Frederick Young. Copyright © 1988 by Thich Tue Sy. Reprinted by permission of Trevor Carolan.

"Lone Pine" and "Tea" by Amy Uyematsu. Reprinted by permission of the author.

"Love after Love" is reprinted from *Collected Poems 1948–1984* by Derek Walcott. Copyright © 1984 by Derek Walcott. Reprinted by permission of Farrar, Straus & Giroux, Inc.

"Yum Yab" is reprinted from *Kill or Cure* (Penguin, 1994) by Anne Waldman. Reprinted by permission of the author.

"Deer Park" by Wang Wei "made new" by C. H. Kwock and G. G. Gach. Reprinted by permission of the translators.

"midnight percussion ..." by Gary Warner. Reprinted by permission of the author.

Mondo by Sojun Mel Weitsman and Zen Center Sangha. Reprinted from *Wind Bell* XIX:2, fall 1986. Reprinted by permission of Mel Weitsman and Zen Center Sangha

"Difficulty Along the Way," "I saw myself ...," "Large Little Circle," "Redwood Haiku," "Small Sentence to Drive Yourself Sane," "Springtime in the Rockies, Lichen," and "Step out onto the planet ..." are reprinted from *Ring of Bone: Collected Poems 1950–1971* by Lew Welch. Copyright © 1979 by Lew Welch. Reprinted by permission of Grey Fox Press. Magda Craig's biographical information about Lew Welch is reprinted from her festschrift *Hey Lew* (Box 964, Bolinas, CA 94924).

"Zen Corners" is reprinted from *33 Fingers: A Collection of Modern American Koans* by Michael Wenger. Copyright © 1994 by Michael Wenger. Reprinted by permission of Clear Glass Publishing.

"The End of the line," "hoist great blocks of language into place ...," "Off. ...," "PET SHOP," and "take dandelions first salad, ..." are reprinted from *Highgrade* (Coyote's Journal) by Philip Whalen. Copyright © 1966 by Philip Whalen. Reprinted by permission of the author. "SATURDAY" by Philip Whalen. Reprinted by permission of the author. "Absolute..." is reprinted from *Wind Bell,* by permission of the author.

"To Papaji" by Nina Wise. Reprinted by permission of the author.

"Loneliness" by Telly Wong. Reprinted by permission of the author.

"Bodhisattva Vow" and "The Update" by Adam Yauch. Reprinted from *Ill Communication* by The Beastie Boys. Copyright © 1994 by Grand Royal/Polygram. Reprinted by permission of Grand Royal/Polygram. Adam Yauch's comments in his biographical information are taken from *Tricycle: The Buddhist Review* IV:4, summer 1995.

"Third Street Promenade; Full Moon, Sunday Night, Santa Monica" by Al Young. Reprinted by permission of the author.

"The Things I Miss" by Paula Yup. Reprinted by permission of the author.

Every effort has been made to locate all rights holders and to clear reprint permissions. If any acknowledgments have been omitted or any rights overlooked, it is unintentional. Please contact Parallax Press with corrections for future editions.

AUTHOR INDEX